INTO THE MIND OF ANOREXIA

INTO THE MIND OF ANOREXIA

Adrienne Vie

Into the Mind of Anorexia

Copyright © 2021 Adrienne Vie

Paperback ISBN: 978-1-946702-56-2

Hardback ISBN: 978-1-946702-59-3

All rights reserved. No part of this book may be reproduced or transmitted in any form or by any means, electronic or mechanical, including photocopying, recording, or by any information storage and retrieval system, without permission in writing from the author.

Published by Freeze Time Media

Special thanks to family and friends who encouraged me to write this book, and my editor who patiently guided me through it.

For all who are living with eating disorders and those who try to help them.

Contents

Introduction	xi
Foundation	xiii
Hilly Lane Farm	1
Seeds	5
Peppermint Schnapps	9
Struggle	17
Labels	19
Secondary Gains	27
Writing Through My Personal Struggle	30
Drawing the Disease	35
Letters	38
Three Minutes of Writing	43
Hypnosis	51
Lifted	53
The Light	55
Gaining Insight	59
Seeing a Vision	73
Guilt	75
Surrender	107
Surrendering Anorexia	108
Psychodrama	114
People on the Psych Ward	120
Jeremiah 29:11	127
The Cleansing	131
Recovery and Relapse	139
Life after Anorexia	146
Accepting Jesus	151
Red Flags	158
Double A	168
Analysis	175
The Psychology of Anorexia	177

Comorbidities and Triggers	183
Coercion and Compulsion	188
Treatment Setting and Approach	192
Medications and Manipulation	198
Self-hypnosis	201
Relearning How to Eat	202
Psychodrama Explained	206
Treatment Challenges	208
Perseverance	211
Relapse	214
Parenting and Eating Disorders	218
Recovery and Growth	224

Introduction

This is the story about my struggle with anorexia nervosa. I've planned to write this book since I was 15 years old. Writing it is part of God's purpose for my life. My journal entries, essays and prayers, and letters sent by other people are included to help you see anorexia nervosa through the eyes of someone who has lived through it. I've included doctor's notes and excerpts from my medical records to describe the physical and psychological effects of the disease.

Most of us know someone with an eating disorder; it might even be you. Whether it is anorexia, bulimia, or obesity, they are very similar. Whether it is an eating disorder, a substance use disorder, an obsessive-compulsive disorder, or any combination of these, I believe that my experiences will resonate with you. God has a purpose and plan for all of us. For me, it is to write this book for you to read. My prayer is that my story will help even one person who reads it. You too can have hope and experience forgiveness despite the choices you make. If you open the door, God will orchestrate miracles in your life.

I included Bible verses because in looking back at my life I can see that God was always present. I encourage you to read these passages in the Bible.

Where does my hope come from? Jesus.

> But in your hearts revere Christ as Lord. Always be prepared to give an answer to everyone who asks you to give the reason for the hope that you have. But do this with gentleness and respect…
>
> 1 Peter 3:15 (NIV)

Foundation

Hilly Lane Farm

As the bus drove past our grid road and on to Mayer's, I felt that familiar lump deep in my stomach start to grow. It wouldn't be long until our stop. My older sister, Catherine, and I were dropped off last when we rode the 56-passenger school bus 18 miles home to the farm. I never really understood that. The bus driver went 20 minutes or more out of his way to make two stops before ours. If we had been dropped off before those kids, it's possible we would have made it to the house at least 20 minutes earlier. That makes a big difference when it gets dark so early in the evening, and when there is stuff to do at home after school. Oftentimes, Catherine and I were both on the bus, but I mostly remember the times when I was alone.

After the Mayer's were dropped off, I sat on the hard, cold, ripped green bench seat and waited for my stop. There was nothing else I could do. Some days we could be dropped off at Aunty Olivia and Uncle Bill's place, which was on the grid road before our far gate. We had mail delivery at the mailbox several miles away two or three times a week. If Mom happened to get the mail on the way home from work or it otherwise made sense, we would get dropped off there and she would pick us up to go home. Aunty Olivia would give us coffee with fresh cream and lots of sugar, and we could watch TV. They had more than the three TV stations that we had at our house. It felt like a real treat. Sunflowers danced in the wind in their farmyard, tall and bright yellow, and their big heads were full of seeds. I loved those days.

But today wasn't mail day, so we drove past Aunty Olivia's and on to the far gate of our farm where the bus stopped, almost a mile from the house. Occasionally Mom was there to pick us up, but usually there was no one. The walk from the far gate to our house didn't bother me. Most of the time my dog, Mickey, waited halfway down the lane for the bus and was ecstatic when he saw it, running back and forth until we reached the house. Seeing my dog was the highlight of the day.

What I dreaded was what happened before that, after the bus stopped at the far gate. The bus driver, John, was a man in his 50s or 60s. He had been our bus driver for as long as I could remember, and to me, he seemed very large and old. Instead of opening the door and letting me off the bus to walk home, he turned off the ignition and unbuckled his lap belt. He turned toward me and started a one-sided conversation. I think the sexual assault began when I was 10 or 11.

When John wasn't driving the bus, he was a farmer. He always wore old, loose, blue canvas pants and a plaid shirt and dusty black shoes. On the days when I was the only kid left on the bus, he would get out of his seat and move toward me to sit on the outside of the seat where I sat at the window. I could not get out of the seat because he was in the way. I couldn't crawl over the seat to the front or back because the bench seat backs were too high. There was nowhere to go to get away anyway because the exit doors were shut tight.

I don't remember John ever kissing me. His large hands started at my waist and moved up under my shirt, cupping and touching my tiny breasts. I tried to push his hands away, but they would not go away. Soon after, his hands and thick fingers with dirty fingernails moved down again and into my pants. His fingers forcefully found and felt his way along as I tried harder to push his hands away and feebly told him "no." I might have started crying once, but I am not sure.

I remember his fingers fumbling and pushing on me. With his other hand he would hold firm to my hand nearest him and push and rub it into his crotch. I could feel his erection, and the bitter sick feeling in my stomach would get worse as I waited for it to end. He had bad breath and smelled like dirt and sweat. At that age, I didn't know what the finish line was or how long it took for him to be done. I don't know if he always ejaculated or if he just got bored and stopped. I know he never stopped despite my protests. I don't even remember if he heard me or said anything at all while he groped me.

I don't know how long it lasted, but it seemed like a long time. Sometimes his pants got wet where my hand was, and I learned that was a sign it would be over with soon. After it was over, John got up and moved back to the bus driver's seat. He opened the large, well-stocked glove compartment and let me select a can of warm soda and a full-size chocolate bar. He also took a can of soda and drank it. I guess that was supposed to be a reward for me, and probably like a cigarette after sex for him. After what seemed like a long time, he finally turned the big handle to open the door and let me out. I left the bus confused, relieved that it was over, and thinking about what would happen for the rest of the week. I clutched my melting chocolate bar and ate it later at home.

This was my horrible embarrassing secret, made worse by the fact that I liked the big chocolate bar that John gave me. I didn't know who to tell or what to do about it for so many years, and even now. What a sad, sick memory to carry around.

One day after it happened and I walked home, I told

Mom. I don't remember how or what made me tell her on that particular day. I do remember her parked and waiting at the far gate to meet the school bus the next day, even though the weather was nice to walk home. John let me out of the bus that day as soon as he stopped at the gate. Mom got out of the truck, marched up to the bus, and then went inside. I sat in the truck and watched them talk, but I couldn't hear what they said. I know Mom was very upset. I could tell by her red face and the way she was waving her arms. When she got back in the truck, I don't remember either of us saying anything more about it. I don't remember if that was the last time John fondled me.

John is dead now, and no, I didn't do it. I'm not sure when or how he died. I feel only numb as I write about this experience. I haven't consciously thought about it for a long time, but I know it has been in my subconscious. I learned how to detach from the present during the experiences just to get through it. With much practice, I became very good at that. Dissociation has been my "go-to" coping mechanism with challenges in relationships and marriages ever since. Decades later, I saw a photograph of me standing in front of the school bus beside John. He was given a bus driver award. I could put myself right back there and see the shameful secret reflected in my expression. I wondered, "Where was God then?"

> My tears have been my food day and night, while people say to me all day long, "Where is your God?"
>
> Psalm 42:3 NIV

Seeds

Growing up on a family farm 18 miles from the nearest town had advantages and disadvantages. The air was clean and the land was beautiful. We had dugouts and small lakes, rolling hills and trees. We always had cows, horses, chickens (one of my favorite animals), pigs, many cats and one or two dogs. Coyotes howled outside my window at night. Magpies and woodpeckers added to the noise in the daytime. I had great fun climbing bale stacks and swinging on ropes in the loft. My sister and I had daily chores, bringing wood from the woodpile for the wood-burning stove and pumping a pail of drinking water from the well and bringing it to the house. They were necessary chores, and I felt a sense of purpose doing them. Between catching field mice and tadpoles, herding chickens, picking berries and riding a pig, I had a great childhood! If you are around my age, you know about the TV series, "Little House on the Prairie." Well, we were more modernized than that, but you get the idea.

There was only me and my sister, Catherine, on the farm. Dad was a farmer and Mom a nurse at the hospital in town. We lived on the prairies and Dad owned way too much land for one man who had no sons to help him. There were rolling fields of wheat, oats, flax, and barley, and pastures with trees, cows, and moose. Nothing interrupted the skyline; the sky extended until it met the ground all around us. Dirt and gravel roads led to and away from our farm on two sides and kept going until they reached town 18 miles away. There were wonderful surprises all over our land. I discovered crocuses, sweet peas and bright orange prairie lilies, and watched amazing hummingbirds, calves being born, and coyotes running freely. I loved riding downhill as fast as I could in the red wagon and swinging on the tire swing.

Mom worked eight-hour rotating shifts at the hospital, and Dad worked as many hours as he needed day and night to keep the farm running. Catherine was more than a big sister to me; she was also a stand-in mom. She cooked, cleaned, taught me how to wash my face, and role-modeled good study habits, including teaching me to love reading by reading to me.

When I was in middle school, I remember Mom trying out diets such as the Medical Diet. I listened to her talk about it and learned a lot. We didn't have computers or any other way to look things up like we do now. Instead, my mom carefully prepared and portioned meals for herself according to the diet.

If I recall correctly, my sister also participated in dieting. I wanted desperately to fit in, so I did too. I couldn't eat the meal with lamb because one of my favorite stuffed animal toys was a lamb. I thought little lambs were so cute and the thought of eating them made me feel ill. Other than lamb, I started carefully measuring and portioning out my food according to the diet we were following. I knew that Mom hid chewy chocolate-flavored diet pills because I would find them in the kitchen cupboards. I didn't know what they were exactly, but since they might make me lose weight and Mom was taking them, I would steal some from the cupboard and eat them myself.

I listened to Mom talk about diets and calories and let it all sink in. It soon became clear to me; the key to happiness was losing weight and being thin. As discussions ensued about how many pounds of weight were lost or needed to be lost, I privately researched how many calories were in all the foods I ate or thought about eating using a little book I had picked up from a grocery store. I tracked all the calories I ate in another little book, overestimating just to be safe. My goal was to decrease to 500 calories per day and stay there.

Mom was a great cook. She made traditional Hungarian dishes that my grandma taught her to make, and she was an incredible baker. She showed love to others by cooking and baking for them. We always had homemade desserts made with our own milk and cream, and we churned fresh butter. We had plenty of muffins and bread in the house at all times, and the freezers were full of meat from our own cattle, chicken, and pigs. There was never a shortage of food at our house.

There were a lot of great years. Holidays were a blast, with many relatives meeting at our farm for days at a time. We spent time snowmobiling, ice skating, and watching my grandma's slide shows from her most recent trips to exotic places around the world. The house was full of laughter and love. All the while I kept my own secrets, monitoring everything I ate, and then secretly heading outside to exercise it off.

My family attended a Presbyterian church where services were done in English as well as Hungarian. When I was not trying to stay awake, I was giggling and talking with my friend between the wooden pews. The family often went for soft ice cream after church, and then drove 18 miles home to eat palacsinta (Hungarian crepes) for lunch. To me, going to church and then getting ice cream was a ritual, as was praying before meals and at bedtime. These rituals were comforting and helped me understand that there was a God who created me. Beyond that, however, I did not understand just how much I was loved.

Personality characteristics such as perfectionism, real or perceived competition with a sibling, physical isolation, an overbearing mother, an absent father, low self-esteem, and a trigger event can push a person over the edge. That's what happened to me.

"Therefore I tell you, do not worry about your life, what you will eat or drink; or about your body, what you will wear. Is not life more than food, and the body more than clothes?"

Matthew 6:25 (NIV)

Peppermint Schnapps

During my fourteenth summer, I stayed with an aunt, my dad's sister. I always thought Aunty Donna was the coolest aunty. I thought she was beautiful. She was very thin with long blonde hair, and seemed full of energy. She smoked cigarettes and weed, the latter of which she grew in her corn patch. With it, she made cookies and rolled her own cigarettes. She also drank a lot of alcohol.

Ironically, she was a psychiatric nurse. At that time, she had already been married and divorced once. I saw her as a free-spirited woman, and I wanted to be just like her. She lived in the biggest city I had ever been to, 100 miles away from the farm. My sister had stayed with her the summer before for a few weeks. I wanted to stay with her then too but wasn't allowed to. I was so envious of Catherine because of that. I have no idea what Catherine did when she stayed there, but I hope it wasn't anything like my stay.

My aunt planned a camping trip for us, and we drove north in her big green car pulling a small trailer behind. We drove up to Pine Lake and parked in the campsite. I had already tried marijuana cookies at my aunt's house before we left, and when we arrived at the campsite, I tried smoking it. It tasted awful and made me nauseous, but the high I felt seemed worth it. I jogged around the campsite, seeing strange, colorful animals in my mind as I ran. When I wasn't running, I sat around the campsite drinking coffee or alcohol and sometimes smoking pot while my aunt jumped up and down from her camp chair, frantically busying herself with trivialities in her usual way.

One evening, two men approached my aunt, asking her to a party. She agreed to go, and I went along. She unhooked the trailer from the car, and we drove around looking for the party beside the lake. When we arrived, there were cars and trucks parked randomly in the dirt near the lake. She parked the car, and we joined the party. I hung around my aunt for part of the time, drinking peppermint schnapps. I was the youngest there by at least five years, as far as I could tell.

After dark, I joined people on the shore who were dropping their clothes and jumping in the lake to skinny-dip. I was terrified but at the same time loved my freedom and the feeling of belonging to a group. Crawling out of the water, I found leaches attached to my skin, and I wildly slapped them away. The party was going strong, and after getting dressed, I found my way back to my aunt and the main group who were standing around a campfire drinking.

A short time later it started raining, and people scattered, running to their cars and ducking into tents and campers as the rain intensified. I ran to the spot where my aunt's car had been parked, only to find it missing. Approaching the remaining partiers, I asked where my aunt was. Someone told me that they thought she had left. I began to get nervous. One of the men who had invited us to the party, the older one, pushed me into a tent and zipped it closed. My memory gets blurry as I try to recall what happened next. I remember feeling very anxious and afraid, with this older man wrapped around me. I remember the smell of peppermint schnapps, the lake and sweat. The inside of the tent was yellow, and there was some light shining in from car headlights outside. I remember struggling, but not being able to get away. I remember the feel of his kisses and his hands on me under my white sweatshirt. Then I woke up.

It was morning and light filled the tent. The rain had stopped, and I felt damp and cold. I heard voices of people outside the tent talking and laughing, and I looked beside me to see a naked man lying there asleep. Looking down, I saw that my white sweatshirt had red stains on it, and my jeans were undone and pulled down. Panic seized me and I frantically tried to clean myself up. Trying to ignore the odd and uncomfortable feeling between my legs, I crawled out of the tent, where people looked at me and then at one another, smiling knowingly. I cannot remember the comments that were spoken, but I felt ashamed and scared. Without a word, I went back to where the car had been parked and again saw the area of dirt where it had been. I stood there, not knowing where to go or what to do. The only person I "knew" was the naked man in the tent. Holding back my tears and nausea, I returned to the group. He was awake and standing among the others, and it took all I had left to ask him if he would drive me to my aunt's trailer.

He agreed, and I got into his convertible. As soon as we started moving I started vomiting both inside and outside his car as he drove to the place where the trailer had been parked before. It seemed to take forever, but when we finally arrived, the car was there. I got out and opened the door of the trailer to find my aunt naked and in bed with a man. It was the other, younger man who had originally asked us to the party. There was blood on the sheets in the trailer. I turned and left the trailer, going to the back of it, and I sat down on the ground, gasping for air. I felt humiliated, dirty, and sick to my stomach. Shortly after, my aunt came out of the trailer. She had gotten dressed. I told her that I wanted to go home, *now*. She scolded me, saying that we need to be "good hosts" to the two men, and make them breakfast. She told me to clean up the inside of the trailer, but I couldn't do it. She made breakfast (bacon and eggs) and served the men as I sat on the ground on the opposite side of the trailer, trying not to vomit.

After they left, we packed up and started driving back to my aunt's house. I don't think I stayed with her any longer after that. I do know that the experience changed my life.

I retreated into myself, changing from a confident, popular, happy teenager to a withdrawn, quiet, introverted shell of a girl. I was drowning in guilt and fear, believing that I had invited the assault, and not knowing what to do about it. I remembered a time when my mom had caught my sister and her boyfriend making out in his truck at the far gate, and how distraught and panicked my mom had been. I was so humiliated and afraid of disappointing her with what had happened to me that I could not tell her, or anyone else. I felt shocked, violated, disgusted, and responsible. I stopped eating and started dropping weight. My periods stopped; I was terrified to disclose what had happened and worried that I was pregnant.

The rest of the summer went by slowly as I re-lived the experience over and over in my head. I hated myself and felt helpless and hopeless. I struggled to find something that made me feel back in control of myself and my world. Having always been active, I ramped up my running miles. I ran a couple of miles once a day on the hilly, wooded dirt roads and cow trails at first, but that gradually turned into running many miles and hours at a time. Even in the winter with snow up to my knees or higher and in temperatures well below zero with wind, I would run or walk miles in complete solitude, trying to escape my dreadful secret.

At the same time, I started dieting to the extreme. I did

my best to count and measure every calorie I ate, keeping the daily calorie count at 500 or less and always overestimating. Because I had grown up in an environment of dieting, I knew what to do. As the pounds fell off my 110-pound frame, I felt a peculiar feeling that the control I thought I had lost was returning, and I craved more of it. Out of the craziness in my world that was out of my control, at least I could control my weight. I grew more and more compulsive with exercise and obsessed with counting calories and recording and managing my food intake. I ignored hunger pains and enjoyed the high I got from low blood sugar. I learned how to eat and drink just enough to keep from passing out. I began to let anorexia nervosa take control of my mind and body. This was at the same time frightening and empowering. Even if the world was out of control, at least I could control something in my life — my weight.

With a small class of 18 or fewer students, my classmates were like brothers and sisters. I had been popular, confident, outgoing, and had dated two or three of the boys in the class as early as grade six. Before that summer I had average grades, terrific friends, a great best friend, and an awesome boyfriend. My sister and her boyfriend sometimes drove me into town on the weekends, and I was exposed to parties and alcohol at an early age. I enjoyed going to "bush parties" with my boyfriend and older kids, where we drank and had the kind of fun that should have waited until an older age, but I was always a "good" girl. When I started ninth grade, however, I was a different person. The classmates I had been with, many since kindergarten, seemed foreign. In my fear and shame, I detached myself from all of them. It all started falling apart as I allowed myself to sink deeper and deeper into the pit that is anorexia nervosa. But, as time passed, a smug confidence grew. While others struggled with their weight, I did not, and I felt superior. I felt like I could run longer than anyone and could diet down to a weight that no one else could reach. That fragile ego is part of anorexia.

Five months after the night in the tent, I reached a point where I knew I had to tell someone what had happened. My periods were gone, and I knew what that could mean; I might be pregnant. Mom and I could always talk about personal things. She seemed to be able to solve every problem...so I told her. Although I have no memory of it, she took me to a doctor who apparently examined me and found that I was not pregnant. Apparently, the doctor announced that "my hymen was intact."

Mom seemed relieved to tell me that, as if that made everything okay. Apparently, I was supposed to feel so relieved too and simply put the whole thing behind me. In certain cultures, there is great value put on virginity and the intact hymen. Realistically, the hymen can show no sign of injury after sexual assault, or it can heal back to its original state. Alternately, it can break with exercise, gymnastics, and horseback riding. It is an unreliable indicator of virginity. The fact that the doctor and my mom were reassured by my apparently intact hymen both confused and nauseated me. If I was not sexually assaulted...then what happened to me? Why did I feel so dirty, guilty, and ashamed? Why had this changed every aspect of my life? Had it only happened in my mind? Did I drink so much that I only imagined that night? I listened silently, holding all my questions inside. No one would understand what I was saying, anyway. No one was there, not even God.

Mom told Dad what happened, and I heard the story secondhand from her. Dad drove 100 miles to my aunt's house to confront her. It was a rare moment when my dad showed emotion, but he was angry. My aunt told him that I should have taken care of myself, and I was old enough to take care of myself. In other words, what happened was my fault and I had asked for it. I internalized that interpretation and carried it around with me all the time. After that, we all seemed to dance around it and each other under a cloud of family secrecy and shame. Maybe if we didn't talk about it, it would go away.

> I live in disgrace all day long, and my
> face is covered with shame
>
> Psalm 44:15 (NIV)

Struggle

Labels

The closest town to our farm was a small prairie town of about 1,000 people. Everyone just about knows everyone, or at least knows of everyone. A person is labeled and recognized for a distinct physical feature, behavior, or association. That became your identity. Anorexia became my identity. I knew it when I walked down the street or went into stores, restaurants, or the hospital where my mom worked. I felt the eyes of other people on me. Early in anorexia, I was proud of my thinning body. At a time when teenagers were growing and developing, I was staying the same and getting thinner.

At some point I no longer controlled anorexia, it controlled me. I became self-conscious and paranoid. I hated going to school or anywhere around other people with their judging eyes and worried frowns. I was happiest when I was left alone at home where I could do what I wanted, when I wanted without criticism, lectures, guilt, or shame. I continually felt like I had and continued to disappoint everyone, especially my mother. Although I knew what to do to reverse anorexia, anorexia was stronger than my rational mind. Anorexia is rooted in anxiety, and research shows that it is closely related to social anxiety. I believe that after my initial pride and fragile vanity associated with thinness passed and anorexia controlled me, I slid into another psychopathology: social anxiety and phobia.

Days at home on the farm during the long winters were very hard. I often went for long runs in the freezing cold and later wondered how I had survived. I would run as hard as I could in the snow, going too far in the strong freezing wind, deep snow, and bitter cold. Sometimes I was not sure where I was or how to get home. Then I would get scared. If I decided not to go outside, I was compelled to find ways to exercise and avoid food in the house.

During one of our long talks at night, Mom told me to start seeing the only doctor in town, and I agreed. When he suggested that I be admitted into the local hospital to get help, I agreed. The thought of being in town (even if I was in a hospital), instead of out on that godforsaken farm in the middle of nowhere sounded good to me. I might finally feel like a "town kid." I would not have to be alone so much, listening to my own torturous thoughts and trying to manage my compulsive behaviors. I was excited and actually felt a glimmer of hope. Part of me thought the time in the hospital could help me recover from anorexia, but another, stronger part of me was not ready to let the disease go.

With socialized medicine, the hospital is used liberally as a type of holding cell for many people. This was especially true in the tiny, 18-bed hospital in town. People with dementia or recovering from a massive stroke were admitted for months at a time, even until they died. Others were admitted when drunk, with anxiety disorders, claiming to be victims of abuse, or all of the above. My sister and I had been born there, and my mom had seen it all in her years there. Everyone knew my mom and she knew everyone. Her reputation was solid as one of the best and funniest nurses in the place. Mom cracked jokes and played pranks on co-workers and danced for old people who smiled and laughed even when they could hardly move or feed themselves. She was an angel in their eyes, and everyone loved her.

I was admitted voluntarily in January at the age of 16.

Mom kept working while I was there. She worked the night shift so that she would not have to be around me as a patient. I cannot imagine the embarrassment she felt at having me admitted with a self-imposed psychiatric disorder in the very hospital where she worked. I only stayed in the hospital for three days. I didn't feel like a "town kid." I felt like a freak. I didn't like being watched, and wanted the freedom of being alone on the farm with no rules but my own.

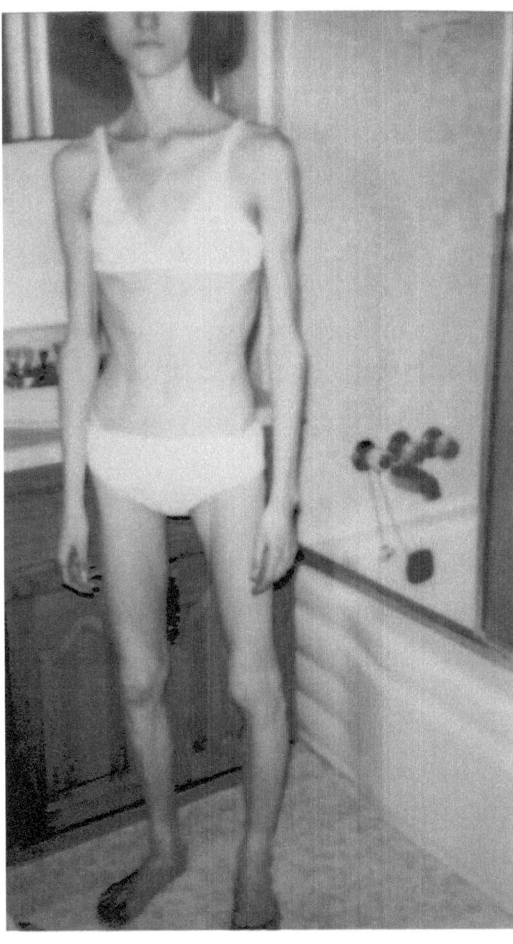

Medical record excerpt, written by Dr. Erickson:

Admitted January 2nd, 1986. Discharged January 5th, 1986

"Presenting Complaint: This patient is suffering from Anorexia Nervosa. She has been attending me regularly in the outpatient clinic for counseling. It would appear that her anorexia developed during the summer of 1984. During this time there were two particular life events which were important to her and anxiety provoking. These events were obviously important to her and initially she did not discuss them readily. These were eventually fully discussed and further discussed with her parents. These discussions appeared to give her some relief and may have been the initiating factors for her anorexia nervosa. Physically her general condition is not good. She suffers from Raynaud's Syndrome, is emaciated, and has lost all of her subcutaneous fat. Her cheeks are hollow. Her schoolwork has been deteriorating and she has lost many of her friends probably because of her physical appearance. She is keen on sports particularly gymnastics and dancing to music and has obviously used the exercise to assist her weight loss.

She has a good understanding of the disease Anorexia Nervosa and also the problems that it is producing for her and her parents. She's an intelligent girl and thoughtful and obviously concerned about the worry she gives to her parents.

She appears to be keen to overcome this problem, but I believe that her mind still has an altered body image and she finds great difficulty overcoming this.

She has been weighing weekly and prior to this admission has been slowly losing weight. She has been keeping a note of her

Labels

daily intake and I have been discussing this with her and supporting her and encouraging her to eat foods of high calorie value. She agreed to this admission as she herself realized that she was not managing to beat this problem at home.

I have been taking a gentle approach with Adrienne and not forcing her to do things against her will as I believe that she has fairly forceful character and force on my part would be met with equal and opposite force.

I discussed the diet with Adrienne and with the dietitian and the plan was that we would try to produce food which she enjoyed eating and that she would do her best to eat it. On admission she initially ate well but her intake gradually decreased during her admission. However, her weight changed from 73.5 pounds to 75 pounds during her admission. On January 5th she was discharged home to return to school. I had hoped that this admission would introduce her to the hospital and demonstrate to her that she had no need to worry about future admissions which I felt were inevitable. She's to be reviewed in the outpatient clinic."

While in the hospital, an overweight, outspoken nurse would try to counsel me about food. As she spoke of how we need to eat to be healthy and described her favorite meals, I watched her talking in her tight uniform with buttons stretched to the limit and thought to myself, "There is no way I will end up looking like her." Yet another reason to let anorexia maintain its control over me.

When I returned home from the hospital, the environment had not changed and neither had I. The loneliness, horrible dark winter days and usual struggles with exercise and diet were still there waiting for me. I knew that as soon as I went back to the farm, I would get worse. A little over a week after being discharged, I voluntarily readmitted myself to the hospital. Again, a small part of me believed that with a little help and a different environment I might be able to someday overcome anorexia. If nothing else, in the recesses of my mind, I knew that in the hospital at least there were people around who could protect me from myself.

Medical record excerpt, written by Dr. Erickson:

Readmitted January 16, 1986. Discharged February 28, 1986

"Adrienne was readmitted after finding it increasingly difficult to manage at home and school. She has become increasingly weak at school and was exercising excessively and eating as little as possible. During this admission she has had frequent counseling during which it has become apparent that she displays almost all of the characteristics typical of a patient with anorexia. She has obsessional tendencies and sets herself forever high targets and becomes equally disappointed when she does not reach them. She has a very competitive nature as exemplified by her constant striving to be as good as her elder sister. All these problems and mechanisms of dealing with them were discussed.

During this admission we initially made up a diet at the beginning of each week consisting of foods which she enjoyed eating and gradually increased the calorie content weekly. The was initially done without counting the calories but later changed to a system in which the diet was made up on an exchange basis with the calories being counted and known and the calorie content being increased by 100 calories weekly. She had obvious difficulty eating her meals and took a long time to eat them.

Her main problem was her compulsion to exercise and this would

Labels

be done whenever possible behind the closed door of her room or elsewhere. She was advised to talk to any of the staff when she felt this compulsion to exercise but she obviously didn't feel happy in doing this. She was then prescribed Diazepam 2mg QID in an attempt to tranquilize her and this had a little success. She was also prescribed sublingual Ativan 1 mg to take to help her relax when she had the compulsion to exercise. Unfortunately, she fought the tranquilizing effects of these drugs and this was often unsuccessful in stopping her compulsion to exercise.

Towards the end of the admission, it was becoming increasingly apparent that a more disciplined approach was required, and plans were made with Adrienne and her parents that she would be discharged on the 28th of February and would attempt to return to school. Her mother is to provide the diet for her using the increasing diet plan made in hospital and she is expected to gain 1 pound per week.

Adrienne realizes that if this method does not succeed then the next alternative would be the anorexia unit in City Hospital. Her weight on admission was 74 pounds and on discharge was 75.6 pounds. Discharge diagnosis: Anorexia Nervosa."

(Dictated but not read or signed as Dr. Erickson left on March 1, 1986.)

In our small town we had doctors who were "locums." That means that foreign doctors rotated through the town for as few as four weeks or as long as a year or two to serve the rural community. Many were young with less than a few years of experience after graduating from medical school. Often the physicians were trained in and from South Africa or another location overseas. It could not have been easy for them in a remote and foreign environment, not knowing what to expect on a day-to-day basis. Serving in this role but having been trained in a different country and having no specialty experience must have been challenging and terrifying at the same time.

Dr. Erickson was the first locum my mom took me to. He was in his thirties, and during his time in town I grew to trust him. I met him in his office in town after school about once a week. I saw it as another chance to be off the farm, and I looked forward to talking with him. He explored the mind of anorexia with me and revealed many thoughts and behaviors associated with the disease that I had not thought about or realized. He was a non-judgmental outsider, and a listening ear when I really needed one. I know that Dr. Erickson gently helped me hit bottom, and for that I am eternally grateful.

After reading his final notes in my chart, I realize that he tried his best to help me but ultimately had to hand me off to my parents because his time as a locum had expired. He understood more about me and my personality than I knew.

> The way of fools seems right to them,
> but the wise listen to advice.
>
> Proverbs 12:15 (NIV)

Secondary Gains

Loosely defined, secondary gains are advantages that occur as a result of an illness, such as extra attention or affection.

<u>Journal entry:</u>

Admitted to Hospital on January 17, 1986

> *I can see that this stay is not going to be easy. I've already been warned not to exercise but I plan to stretch in my bathroom anyway and do my 50 sit-ups at night on my bed. Today I had one-half slice of toast with butter, 1 glass of unsweetened pineapple juice, 1 glass of milk, 1 serving of rice Krispies, one-half cup of creamed cottage cheese, 1 muffin, and 1 orange.*
>
> *I don't know what they serve for supper; all I know is that it comes very early, which is okay, I guess. All the more time to work it off before bed. I want to see Peter. I miss him badly. I wish he would have phoned, but I don't think he did last night. God, please don't let him forget about me and drop me. I need him. Let him be patient and understanding and caring.*
>
> *I enjoy the meals here because they give me what I want for dinner, which is pressure off of me.*
>
> *I'm happy to start a journal because in it, I can draw, paint, color, and write away to my heart's content. Today Mom and Dad are going to come and visit me and bring in my art course. Mr. Smith spoke to the class today and told them about me.*

I'm so glad. He also talked to the teachers about me this morning. I will write the English final, the Home Economics final, and I should write physics and algebra too. I have to bring my grade up somehow!

Walter just came in! I had a nice talk with him. I got a card! Kate came in and we had a good talk. She gave me a card and a rose bowl. Mom and Dad came in and brought everything I needed. Cara and Sonny came also. I had an excellent talk with Cara. I got my Christmas pictures back, some new magazines, and letters from my sister and my aunt. "Golden Girls" came on at 6:30. I'm phoning home at 7 to see about tomorrow night. Then I'll phone Peter. I hope to go home tomorrow. I had a nice supper! Soup, 1 glass of milk, 1 open-faced bun with one-half slice cheese and one-half slice ham on one-half. Salmon salad on the other half. One small pickle, 1 apple. It was good! My science teacher came, and Peter phoned! I can probably go home tomorrow night! I wasn't pressured for lunch!!

People with anorexia are starving for attention. The responsiveness I received in the hospital from staff and visitors seemed to supply all my needs. Sometimes any attention is better than no attention, even if it is for the wrong reasons. However, over time I went from feeling like a celebrity to feeling like a zoo animal. I'm sure most people hoped I would recover and not die trying. When I wrote that journal entry, I had eaten, drank, and was feeling high from enough sugar in my blood, but the good feelings were temporary. As soon as time passed, the old feelings of anxiety returned and I reverted back to anorectic behaviors. The secondary gain one experiences from having a mental health disorder, even self-imposed, can make it seem worth holding on to. The main benefit of being hospitalized was that I was not back on the farm in isolation, just trying to make it through the day. This option seemed better.

The obsessive-compulsive behavior that coincides with anorexia nervosa was apparent in my journal entries. My thoughts were always on food, drink, calories, and planning to get rid of them. I prayed to God, but the prayers were purposefully shallow, empty, and lacking in sincerity. I didn't want God; I still wanted anorexia.

My journaling at this point in time sounded histrionic. While that came through in my writing, it did not show to others. I was in fact very secretive. My behavior was secret, and to everyone except Dr. Erickson, my thoughts were secret too. My main competitor was in my own mind. Beginning stages of anorexia include feelings of anxiety, low self-esteem, and desire for the admiration and attention of others, clouded by the quest for perfection. As the disease takes hold, fragile vanity and pride come with it. Later emotions include guilt, anxiety, depression, and apathy. Anorexia nervosa is an internal battle and, like other types of addiction, will persist and control you unless you are able to completely surrender it.

> Be sober-minded; be watchful. Your adversary
> the devil prowls around like a roaring
> lion, seeking someone to devour.
>
> 1 Peter 5:8 (ESV)

Writing Through My Personal Struggle

My own obsessive thoughts about food and exercise even scared me sometimes. Journaling helped me express them in a way I thought would be safe.

Journal entry:

January 19, inpatient, grade 11, 16 years old:

> Went home yesterday (on an overnight pass), and the stereo was out of my room. Before leaving the hospital I just about went snake waiting for dad to pick me up. Terry stayed with me four hours! We went for walks. She thought I was crazy. Got home and changed clothes. Peter, John, and Anna came over. I drank half of a vodka and 7-Up. Good talk with Peter. Supper was hard. Small glass of wine, creamed salad, pickles, small potatoes, very small stuffing, little fried chicken, peas. Did not eat most of it. Mom gave me a HUGE piece of pie. I asked for a little, but she didn't listen. I only ate half. I finished those drinks. I had about a half of a beer. Watched TV and played games. Had coffee and a half piece of zucchini loaf. Peter and I made out until about 3:30 a.m. I had a little wine. We care about each other. I got up this morning at 8 a.m. Had one piece of toast, little butter (75 calories). Mom gave me two pieces and I left one. Coffee. Peter went to church with Mom and Dad and

I went back to the hospital.
First day on pills (Valium), kind of high feeling.

I knew that having the stereo in my bedroom at home was a trigger to exercise, so I told my doctor who asked Mom to remove it. I felt relieved. Even looking at it compelled me to exercise.

Peter was at least two years older than me and from a nearby town. I'm not sure how we met or how he came to like me. I was a scarecrow and could not have been pleasant to hug, hold, or kiss, but I quickly learned that some men like that. I didn't care who liked me, as long as someone did. I needed to feel that life was worth living, and he helped me feel that way. I also started finding ways to get the attention and appreciation from a man that I did not get as a child. In the back of my mind, I knew my dad loved me, but he never told me that I was pretty. In fact, my first childhood memory was when I was 4 or 5 years old. I colored a picture and showed it to Dad when he came inside after a long day of working on the farm. I loved coloring and tried hard to make my pictures perfect. Mom, as usual, bubbled over telling me how beautiful she thought the picture was. I had heard that so often I was deaf to it. What really mattered was Dad's approval. I proudly showed it to him. He looked at it and said, "That's not very nice," and he pointed to places where I had colored outside the lines. I was crushed. At the time I didn't know that my grandpa spoke to my dad in that way, and he was just repeating what he heard from his own father.

I didn't want Peter to think I was too weird, so when I was with him I tried not to be. I tried to be normal. I tried a little bit harder to eat and drink like everyone else. In my rigid world, I did not drink alcohol because I knew it reduced inhibitions, and that could mean I would eat things that I otherwise would not. For that reason, I was afraid of alcohol and stayed away from it, but I wanted Peter to like me, so I drank it when I was with him, and then made out with him. I felt dead inside but managed to act as expected. We didn't have intercourse because the closer we got to it, the more dead I felt. Although I said nothing, I know he could see my apathy and it made him stop.

Journal entries:

January 20, local hospital 1986

> *For breakfast I gave back the egg and got cereal. I had one piece of toast and one glass of milk over cereal. Dinner was good. I had cottage cheese, cheese, veggies, and my muffin, some veggies, and some mushrooms. I am supposed to drink a lot.*
>
> *Strangest heartbeat last night. Will I be weighed today? I threw most of the small shake away, but I tasted it.*
>
> *Get to have chicken sandwich for supper. Hope it's good. Yuck! Got pineapple juice instead of grapefruit! Not going to drink it. For supper two pieces of toast as chicken sandwich. Salad and cottage cheese. Half of a banana. Glass of juice. I got hungry later tonight and had one apple and two chocolates. My weight is 74.8 pounds today.*

Monday January 27, 1986

> *Good day. Thank goodness for these pills. Easy breakfast of one piece of toast and cereal. Kind of dizzy and high. I don't really like my hair. I wish it was longer. I kind of mellow out on these pills. On Saturday, Mary, Joan, and Sarah showed up and gave me three roses. I'm glad I went home on a pass.*

I talked to Catherine; she's coming home on Valentine's Day. She sounds good; I love her. For dinner I got a nice salad and nuts. It was excellent. For supper I got chili on a taco shell, green beans, half of a piece of bread, and a muffin for dessert. I helped myself to another. I'd like to be out of here by next Monday if at all possible. I'm positive for a job at the lake! I can hardly wait! I'd rather not know what my weight is. I hope nobody tells me, please. Hope I get visitors tomorrow. Got another pill before bed. That's good. I even remembered to say my prayer before eating. I'm happy and content today. I hope Wendy isn't working any more. She pressures me. I will have a bath in the morning. It will feel good. Mom's going shopping tomorrow. She made me good muffins today. Thank you, Lord, for such a terrific mom. She's getting me a crisp meat burrito! I'll save the burrito until Wednesday night for supper. I enjoy food now, as long as it is fixed the way I like. I have to enjoy it. I need to try to sit down more tomorrow, but I prefer to stand. It is good that Dr. Erickson gives me some discipline. I think I almost love him too. I'm kind of buzzed. Oh well!

Tuesday January 28, 1986

Only Tuesday. Difficult day. My mind is really screwed. Started okay. Got up, showered, cleaned up, changed, had breakfast; bowl Rice Krispies, 1 glass milk, 1 pc toast with one slice cheese on it. I ate the cereal, threw the cheese, and burnt the toast and threw the crusts. I figured then I'd be hungry for lunch. Well, I exercised quite a bit and I was hungry.

Dora and Barb came to see me. Lunch showed up. It was ugly. I got upset. Nobody told me it wouldn't be the usual. I was very angry. Loretta told me that is what Dr. Erickson said. He never told me. I demanded to go see him, so we went to his office and talked. I got my way with the "snack lunch" but to increase it daily. I'll do that. I had salad with oil and vinegar dressing, muffin, 1 slice cheese, and cheesecake. It was good. Leslie the RN came and talked to me. She is very nice. Finished one art picture. Exercised more. Walked downtown. Dinner was steak and shrooms, corn, potatoes. Left part of it. Did little exercising. Did more art. Phoned Peter.

Saw Mom downtown. Was "out of touch" in the store. Strange feelings. It is 9:39 and I'm ready for bed. Not getting any better. Boring. Have to get up tomorrow and have nice hot bubble bath. I was scared and very upset at noon. Very, very upset. I wish my mind wasn't so screwed. On the next page I draw it like it is. GOD, PLEASE HELP ME.

In the same way, the Spirit helps us in our weakness. We do not know what we ought to pray for, but the Spirit himself intercedes for us through wordless groans.

Romans 8:26 (NIV)

Drawing the Disease

This was the first time I drew "THIS THING." Anorexia nervosa. The disease was its own entity at this point, and it controlled me. A very powerful, frightening devil. I had grown depressed, exhausted, and apathetic. Staying the same was far easier than trying to fight anorexia. This drawing illustrates how I was torn between the support of Dr. Erickson and the pull of anorexia. It was clear that they were on opposite sides of the battle, with me in the middle, being pulled equally from both sides. I am skeletal and pathetic in contrast to anorexia. In the original, anorexia is positioned at the bottom of the picture, closer to its origin, which I believe is Hell. It has devil ears, an open, screaming mouth, and a heavy waistline. When I was alone, overwhelmed, and feeling out of control, I saw anorexia, and it looked like this. This picture still makes my stomach upset.

I was close to my darkest time, and the compulsions of anorexia had taken hold. It seemed as though no one was watching me while I was in the hospital. I was exercising as much as possible and eating and drinking as little as possible. Even water was almost forbidden; I knew it was good for my body and I needed it, but anorexia convinced me that I was worthless and too far gone, so I avoided it. I knew the small-town hospital routines well enough. There was no one in the kitchen at night, and the staff was scarce. I slipped out of my hospital room with the muffin Mom had brought me, and quietly creeped downstairs to the empty, dimly lit kitchen and put the muffin in the toaster oven. I cranked the toaster oven on full-blast and listlessly watched the muffin turn brown and black as it burnt. I felt dead inside like the burnt muffin. Charred and worthless. I wanted the food, but anorexia was in control. I would not allow myself to have the muffin unless it was so badly burned that it was hardly edible. I knew my thoughts and actions were out of control, but I could do nothing about it.

When I started to see smoke, I opened the toaster oven and reached in with bare hands. My wrists made contact with the inside of the oven door and I felt pain as my skin burnt. Finally… I felt something! The pain jarred me, and I was instantly alert. I could feel my skin begin to blister and watched it in quiet amazement. The experience thrilled and frightened me at the same time. It was so good to feel something — anything. Pain gave me a rush, but even then, I knew it was a slippery slope. I knew that deliberate self-harm would provide only fleeting satisfaction and I would be left empty and scarred with even bigger problems. I knew that I would desire to feel something — even pain — again and again and it would snowball into addiction. I had discovered temporary relief by self-treating my emotional pain by inflicting physical pain. Although I decided to never do that again, I kept the experience a secret and thought about it often, remembering how it felt and wanting to feel alive like that again.

> Night and day among the tombs and in the hills
> he would cry out and cut himself with stones.
>
> Mark 5:5 (NIV)

Letters

Word that someone is in the hospital travels fast in a small town. Loving, concerned, and probably also curious friends and family wrote letters trying to help me. These are the letters.

Letter from my sister:

> *I phoned home this morning and Mom and Dad said that you were still in the hospital. How is it going? Adrienne, you are just going to have to make up your mind to be normal again and go back to a life that holds so much promise and love for you. Not a hospital where you are totally dependent and sheltered from the outside world. I know you are strong, determined and can win over this disease — but you have to try. Just eat and make yourself refuse to exercise even if you feel so terribly guilty; that stage will pass as your obsession with food and exercise changes — it must change. Please write and tell me how you are doing. I wish I could come home and visit but my break is soon so I will see you then. With undying love and care.*

This letter fell on deaf ears. I was not receptive to what Catherine was saying at the time, but the statement about underlying guilt was right. Saying "just eat and make yourself refuse to exercise" makes it seem like I could just say "Okay." This might have been an option during the first year of the disease, but anorexia was stronger than I was when I received this letter. Anorexia controlled me like a puppet master works his puppet. Catherine was pursuing a bachelor's degree in nursing. Her comment about the inverse relationship between obsessions and compulsions and improved nutrition and hydration was correct, but I was not ready to surrender the disease yet. I was grateful for the shelter, security, and predictability of the hospital. Without boundaries, anorexia was completely in control. In the hospital, I could manipulate some rules, but many were non-negotiable. That comforted me. Maybe the whole world was not as out of control as I thought.

Letter from Catherine's friend Anne:

Surprise! How are you doing? Now is that a typical question or what? I'm so afraid of saying the wrong thing so maybe I should just tell the truth. I heard from Shelley that you are not doing too well. That really hurts me to hear that because you are such a beautiful person and so many people love you. Why don't you love yourself? You are one of the kindest people I know. I remember when you would always make sure that Beth, your rabbit, had enough food or that she was warm enough. And I swear, you and your mom probably showed more love to the elderly patients in the hospital than anyone I know could have. And how about when you would always bring my family homemade chocolates at Christmastime? And, of course, your teachers would get some also. I wish that half the compassion you have for others could be directed to yourself because you deserve it. What more can I say? You are so very special. Please take care of yourself. I love you, and I love your family. I don't want anything to happen that would cause pain to anyone in your family. Even though

> *I'm far away, I can be as close as a phone call or a letter. Please take care and also say hi to your parents for me. Thanks. Love, Anne.*

Anne was our minister's daughter. She was one of those people who glowed. She was always happy and smiling. It is awesome that she thought to write me when I was sick. It's unfortunate that at the time I received the letter, I just put it with the others. I didn't believe that I was special or worthy of anyone's letters or love. I was not ready to be helped. I was numb reading the letter, and then filed it away. However, the direct approach used writing this letter made me keep it. She struck a nerve.

Letter from my cousin Jane:

> *Hi, cuz. I've started this letter four times trying to decide what to say to you and how to say it. I decided there's no point in going into great detail right now about what has happened in my life that reminds me so much of yours. The one thing I know is that even though we're on different sides of the "scale" we are an awful lot alike and have been through a lot of the same things. I guess what I'm asking is do you want to talk to someone who understands and cares an awful lot about you? I've always thought about you as being very special and I want you to know I'm here for you and there's not much you could tell me that I have not experienced in my own life. If you want to write me back, I will tell you about some of the less than wonderful events that have happened in my life and how I have and have not coped with them. You are not alone in what you feel, and I am hoping maybe we can help each other. Please write soon. Love, Jane.*

I never wrote Jane back. I never felt close to her, but this might have been an opportunity to be. I know I read this letter, but I was not ready for help. I saved it, however, so I know Jane reached me and I wanted to hold on to the option to reach out to her. I was afraid to hear another person's problems when I didn't even know how to cope with my own.

Letter from a classmate:

> *Hi! I got your letter and I read that pamphlet. It is very interesting. I hope you built up your strength and put on at least 10 or 15 pounds. I didn't want to tell you this but ever since we've been friends, everyone keeps asking me if you put on weight. I said no but I wish she would at least a little anyway. Everyone still cares for you. They are hoping for the best for you. I don't know if they know you are in the hospital.*
>
> *I was starting to get mad at you for the way you were acting, but when I read that pamphlet I understood. Before you lost all the weight that you did, I thought you were just right: human, feminine, just like it says in the pamphlet. I watched a show last night called "Just the Way You Are." The theme was that you should be accepted how you are. You should not have to worry about a boyfriend saying "a few pounds of fat." You should be happy and jolly however you are inclined to be. I'm glad you had fun at the dance. I'll see you at school. I'll give you your pamphlet back. Luv, Terry.*

Terry was one of the few "friends" I had left. I wanted so badly for her to understand this disease and understand me, so I gave her a pamphlet about people with eating disorders. Even in my foggy mind, I knew that knowledge is power.

> Therefore encourage one another and build each other up, just as in fact you are doing.
>
> 1 Thessalonians 5:11 (NIV)

Three Minutes of Writing

I am eternally grateful to my high school English teacher who encouraged us to write every day for three minutes. While at first I thought it was stupid and was uncomfortable doing it, I came to look forward to it. I used it as a way to express my thoughts and feelings and not be judged for them. If I didn't put them on paper, they remained stuffed deep down inside.

September 9, 1986:

Tomorrow I go see the doctor in town. His name is Dr. Harry and he is really good with me. I have to get weighed. I wish everything would be in a more normal set pattern every day. I wish I wouldn't always get bored and anxious when I go home. I have to be 90 pounds tomorrow or I can't start volleyball yet. I'd love to begin it already because I need the practice and I don't want to be a benchwarmer. I don't want to be home alone this weekend because I might go snake at home trying to find something to do. I don't want to gain the weight quickly because then I'll just lose it. When I don't do well, I get drowsy and sleepy. My stomach hurts. It's really weird feeling this way. I feel so hot; maybe I am sick.

September 11:

Today isn't a very good day, but I guess it could be if I want it to be. Why does it bug me to think about what I will do after school? I wish it wouldn't bug me. These jeans are really ugly. I knew darn well that Mom would say they "look good." Maybe they do, I don't know, but they feel lousy. I don't think the waist is the right size. Mom and I bickered about my getting a ride to the bus this morning. I want to say sorry when I get home. I hope I'm good at volleyball this year. I love my art course and can hardly wait until they send back the results of it. I want to go to college next year.

September 15:

Today is a strange day. It is Monday. Starting yesterday, I am getting on normal eating habits. Mom is helping me. I need it. It is very hard to do. I have not done it for so long. Yesterday was a 5K run. I had to leave my friend behind because she was going too slowly. I jogged non-stop 3 kilometers into town. The other stretch I walked and jogged as well. I'm proud to know I can last 3 kilometers without stopping. I felt so good after! I was tired though. I was 87 and a half pounds on Friday. That is less then I was the week before. Better luck next time!

September 17:

Today may be a good day. Mom and I are working on a new strategy for me to get normal. I go see the doctor on Friday. I wish I could play volleyball this weekend. I don't know what to do this weekend. Maybe go to the show. Probably stay home. I'm not sleeping well. I didn't get along well with Cara and Krista on the bus this morning and I almost fought with another person. I need to get everything organized. Today Mom is picking me up after school. It's going to be boring at noon today. There's never anything to do. I have to go for my walk early tonight if I want to get it in, which I do. I have to feel normal. No more art course for a while.

September 18:

>I'm trying to fit in and be liked, but it's not that easy. I don't get along very well with others. I wish I could. I don't know what to do. I wish I could go in volleyball because then I could be with people more and have a good time more and not always be at home. I guess the best thing to do this weekend is go to the city on Saturday. At least I won't go snake being home, bored and alone. There is nothing to do, really. Just dig potatoes and carrots and turnips and cut dill, but I love doing that work. I loved the walk me and Mom took last night. She is such a beautiful person and I love her! I wish I had a boyfriend but I think that's just a dream. I wish I could get in more of a pattern with meals, but I haven't since last time I wrote. I would still like to try and never give up. It's so important. I have to look at priorities and get them done first.

September 19:

>I have to go to the doctor today after school. If I am 90 pounds, I can start volleyball next week. I hope I am. Everything is okay at home. It's not so bad anymore. I have to take control and handle my own life. I have to ask the doctor what to take because I am constipated. How do I arrange meals so I don't gorge at night, yet not be too different from what I eat now? I need help that way, I think. I hope I won't need to wait in the doctor's office for one hour before seeing him. What should I do this weekend? I want to go to the city tomorrow if Mom is not working. Otherwise, I will go snake at home. I

wish I had a boyfriend. I didn't fight with anyone on the bus today.

September 24:

Hello. Today is Wednesday. Today might be a good day. I hope Mom goes to the city today. I don't know why I want her to go, I just do. It's strange. Dad gave me heck about running at night, but he doesn't know I've been doing it for years already. Mom knows now, too. I don't want her to be mad at me. We have a social studies test today. I don't know how good I will do. Please, Lord, help me to do well, because it is so crucial to my being accepted into college. Help me to grow up a lot before then. I have to learn to take care of myself and be good to myself. Help me to grow up. I want to like myself enough to want to help myself. Maybe I like myself too much and that's the problem. I am just babbling today. It's not a good day to write like this. I'm going to sleep if it is ugly out when I get home after school.

September 29:

Today I got to talk to Mom for the first time since Thursday morning. She was away visiting Aunty. I thought she would buy yogurt sesame chips. I wanted them because they have no salt, fat or oil, just good stuff. Instead, she bought a bunch of junk food, chocolate and peanuts. I don't need that. I've got to get away from it. I have to have things that are good for me! It's so hard sometimes at night, and I don't need junk food. I'm just going to get fat and as big as a house. I don't know what to do. Today I will go buy some Melba squares. I'm not going to touch that stuff Mom bought. **I'm not going to touch that stuff Mom bought.** *I love Mom and everything, and I'll tell her what I think, and I will say sorry, and everything. I* hope she won't be hurt. I love her so much. Last night I wrote a five-page essay. I handed it in today. I cannot let anyone read it — yet.

October 6:

Today I go see the doctor after school. Why couldn't I keep away from that bloody scale at Catherine's? No wonder she turned it off. I weighed 87 pounds once, and 91 pounds another time. What do I weigh now? Who knows? I just hate not knowing. I wish I wasn't so moody sometimes. I wish Mom would not dote on me so much, like this morning. It makes me feel so guilty and not worthy of her love. I was out of control with food on Friday night. Saturday wasn't bad — just popcorn and licorice. I think Catherine was mad at me Sunday because I did not eat what she made. She made sandwiches but I had a muffin instead. So big deal. But she was probably hurt. I love her so much and just want to please her.

October 7:

Today is the day, like I told Mom, that I am going to eat normally. I was 86 pounds, down from 90 pounds last week, supposedly. Last week I had a drink before I went to get weighed. Today I only had half of a grapefruit, a burnt muffin, a kiwi, and a crabapple. Isn't that sick. I only had coffee to drink. I don't know why I burnt the muffin; I only know that I like it that way ever since I burned food in the hospital. I remember sticking things in a toaster oven until they were nearly on fire, or actually were. I hope someday I will write about that part of my life. In a way, I am looking forward to it. I have to get better or Mom and Dad won't let me go to college. I'm still sick. It was nice running in the dark last night though! I'm just glad no one saw me. I hope it gets nice today so I can go again.

October 22:

Everything is going okay. I think I am just tired. I can't see very well. I might need stronger contact lenses. Lori just gave me back my textbook. Not a word was said. Sarah did not even say "hi" to me this morning, even when I was the only one in the room. I wish I could get a good grade back or something today to brighten up my day. First gymnastics class tonight.

October 23:

I don't know what to write about today. Gymnastics went well last night. I just have to keep busy. I hope to get everything straightened out this week. I am running, but I am eating normally now. I save my desserts until later in the evening. I have tea if I want something. It worked great last night! I got so much homework done as well and all the cleaning I wanted, too. It was good. Thank you, Lord. I hope tonight will go as well. I have lots to do. I go to the doctor tomorrow. I hope I am 90 pounds like last week. That would really make me happy. I wish I knew if I was exercising too much. I hope not. I hope I have not dropped below 89 pounds again. I can't really tell. My body isn't really letting me know. I feel so good and strong, though.

I disclosed private thoughts and feelings to my high school English teacher via "3 minutes of writing," and received encouragement rather than criticism. After that, it felt safe to spill more into an essay.

Three Minutes of Writing

Twelfth grade essay 1986:

Over the past two years I have experienced a kind of personal suffering. I know what it is from in part. That is what this essay is about.

All through high school — from grade 6 through grade 9 — I have had a very easy life. Everything seemed to be handed to me on a silver platter. I don't want to sound like I am bragging, but I have been told that I had it all: boyfriends, looks, clothes, all the things that are so important in a teenager's life. I was so happy and decent grades were not a problem to achieve. I thought I had everything going for me too, and it reflected in the way I acted towards other people. My opinion of myself was that I was pretty terrific. Really hot. Nothing could knock me down. I was proud of having a steady boyfriend when no one else my age did, and I forgot all my other friends and really hurt quite a few of them. I looked down on most other people and thought I was way above them.

But over the course of about a year, things slowly began to change. A number of reasons all added together made this possible. I broke up with my boyfriend, lost many friends, was away from home a lot, and was forced into growing up before I was ready because of certain occurrences. Also, I lost a close friend, and developed a compulsion to be perfect. I never realized the effect this had on me. If I would have known what I would be like now, two years later, I would have done something back then.

Different situations and pressures affect different people in many ways. Maybe through alcohol, maybe drugs, an maybe taking it out upon yourself, maybe making yourself suffer. I think that's what I've been doing for the past two years.

I have learned a lot about being on the receiving end of comments, ridicule, and sarcasm now, when before, I was the one dishing it out all of the time. I wish I could take back all the crap I handed out to everybody all of my life and help them know that I understand things better now. I guess, in a way, now I am paying for the bad things I have done.

But how long will it be before I get to stop paying? I sure hope it is soon. I know that I'm the only one who can help myself, but that is the most difficult part. You cannot realize the pain of others until you have experienced that type of pain yourself. I'm able now to sense other people's feelings much easier and relate to them.

Pity is the last thing I want, and I don't like looking and feeling weak, because I know that weak people never get anywhere in life, and I have a big life planned ahead of me. I hope that now I can continue that life without too many problems, because time goes by much too fast to waste it trying to sort out your own problems, when you could be helping others sort out theirs.

My English teacher commented that she was "flattered" that I shared this paper with her. She probably knew that sharing these thoughts and feelings helped me more than I can express. Her brief words of encouragement kept me writing and helped me see that it might be okay to share my pain with someone else.

Whoever conceals their sins does not prosper, but the one who confesses and renounces them finds mercy.

Proverbs 28:13 (NIV)

Hypnosis

I continued to have appointments with the locum doctors that came and left town. I went to the doctor's office after school for one hour, once a week. One doctor had dark eyes and hair, thick eyebrows, a deep voice and a shadowy demeanor. To me, he looked mysterious and a little bit scary. When he told me that he was able to hypnotize people, I was both afraid and excited. During one appointment he was able to hypnotize me. When I was under, he asked me to tell him about the time I was sexually assaulted in the tent. When he brought me out of hypnosis, I was crying, shaking, sweating, and spent. He told me what had happened during that session and showed me a cassette player, telling me that he had taped the session. Then he pulled the cassette tape from the device and threw it hard across the room into the garbage can. He told me to do that with the memories I had shared with him. The session amazed me. I wanted and tried to do as he said, but I was only able to stuff the memory into the back recesses of my mind. It was still there.

> It is better to take refuge in the Lord
> than to trust in humans.
>
> Psalm 118:8 (NIV)

Lifted

The Light

In the days before Christmas of December 1986, I was in a state of panic. Relatives, including my Aunt Donna and her husband, my sister, and my grandparents were coming to the farm to celebrate Christmas with me and my parents. There would be a lot of food, the expectation to eat, and pressure from everyone. How would I be able to escape outside and go for my long walks and runs? How would I be able to dodge meals with everyone? How will I be able to resist the food and desserts I used to love but now will not allow myself to eat, except for sometimes, in secret? I dreaded the upcoming holiday and my anxiety grew more each day. Frantically, I increased time spent exercising, and ate even less in the days leading up to their visit.

Around this time, Mom told me that she couldn't fight my disease anymore. She could no longer help me. I know she had trouble at her job, and probably just getting through each day. I felt completely responsible and overwhelmed with guilt. Even I knew she had exhausted herself giving all she could to help me, and now she was giving up. I felt relieved because I didn't want to drag her with me through my hell anymore.

I lay in bed one night in the darkness, unable to sleep because of gnawing hunger, stomach pain, coldness, or vivid nightmares. My hipbones ached where they gouged into the mattress. I felt sharp pains in my chest that frightened me. I knew why I felt this way. I knew that I could not go on forever like this, but that didn't frighten me. As usual, I repeated the same hollow bedtime prayer to myself that I had been saying for as long as I could remember: "Now I lay me down to sleep, I pray the Lord my soul to keep. If I should die before I wake, I pray the Lord my soul to take. Amen." This time, however, was different. I thought about death, not with fear and dread, but with peaceful, calm consideration. For the first time, I opened my mind to the presence of God, and really spoke to Him. I knew He was there. I had known it the whole time. I knew He would heal me, and I was ready to accept His gift.

With my eyes, heart, and mind wide open, I prayed to God to either let me die now, or to get me well, because I could not go on like this anymore. As soon as I spoke the prayer, a brilliant yellow light filled my bedroom. I felt a warmth unlike anything I had ever felt come over me, like a warm water wash, and a feeling of peace that I had never experienced before. I knew it was an answer from God. Suddenly my mind was crystal clear; I knew He was going to heal me. I had surrendered the disease to Him, and He lifted it from me without delay. Immediately, I called out for Mom. She came to my room, and I told her to put me in the hospital *now*. I knew I didn't have much time left to live, but that God wanted me alive, so it was time for action.

As I lay in my bed, I remember hearing Mom talking on the phone, trying to find a place for me. City Hospital, 300 miles away, was one of the places she called, and they agreed to admit me a few days later. I fell into a peaceful sleep.

As I waited for the day to arrive, in the same way that an overweight person limits food and fluids before a Weight Watchers weigh-in, I maintained my obsessive-compulsive exercise habits and food restrictions. Even with the knowledge that God was going to heal me now, the disease still controlled my behavior. Eating, drinking, and exercise habits were so ingrained that I didn't know what else to do. I was controlled by compulsions in the same way as a compulsive gambler, alcoholic, drug addict, or anyone addicted to computer games, food, or sex. I had to continue. There was no other choice. I was convinced that my world would collapse if I didn't. But those days were very different for me inside my heart. The continual state of anxiety that I had grown used to was gone. God had replaced it with absolute calm. I knew that somehow, some way, the disease would be conquered. It was time to give it up. I knew that my life had a purpose.

Those days, and many before that, are hazy memories. I was in a state of starvation, dehydration, and electrolyte imbalance. I was cold all of the time and had mysterious intermittent aches and pains in my chest, abdomen, and legs.

When the day to be admitted into the hospital arrived, Dad was designated to drive three hours to take me there and drop me off. Mom and Catherine were home at the time, but I learned later that they felt like they could not hold it together enough to take me. Dad *always* held it together. Shortly after I said goodbye to Mom and Catherine and we drove away, I realized that I had forgotten something so Dad drove me back to the house. I remember entering the kitchen and knowing I had caught Mom and Catherine off-guard. I don't recall what they were doing, but tension was thick in the air. Later, I learned that they thought I had changed my mind.

I literally perched in the seat as Dad drove me in his usual silence. He is a man of few words, but when he does speak, people listen. He is observant, and always thinks before he speaks. I admired those qualities and always hoped I would also be that way. I only saw Dad mad two times that I remember. Once, a cow died. It had gotten into the chop granary and literally ate itself to death. Dad came in the house, opened the door into the kitchen, and threw his gloves across the room. Another time it was hailing outside and his crops were getting pulverized. He was looking out the screen door in the porch, swearing in Hungarian. That's it.

And the peace of God, which transcends all understanding, will guard your hearts and your minds in Christ Jesus.

Philippians 4:7

Gaining Insight

Almost as soon as I arrived at the hospital, I started journaling. Self-exploration had begun.

December 29, 1987

> Dad drove me up to the hospital by 4:30 p.m. yesterday. I slept pretty well. I met some nice girls last night. I have to stay in my room, but that's okay. I will be able to watch TV in a few days; probably I can write and draw, so I'm going to write a kind of summary of some things I did at the small-town hospital because they bug me so much and I feel so guilty about them and want to get them off my chest. I'm not going to do any of those things here because they scare me so much. I don't want to do anything behind the nurse's backs like in the small-town hospital. I'm glad I can draw and write. If they want me to write what I'm feeling, I will, no problem. I have to start trying on and wearing my new and older jeans so I can get used to the feel of them and break them in. Tomorrow I will wear my new jeans and a shirt tucked in. Today I had blood tests and an ECG, and I spoke with two doctors and a dietitian.

Standardized Questionnaires

Along with several physical examinations, I was asked

to complete standard questionnaires. I felt that I had nothing left to lose, so I might as well be honest. Responses to the *Anorexia and Bulimia Self-Report Questionnaire* provide insight into the thoughts and behavior of people who have an eating disorder, and helped me identify my own.

I stated that I was generally happy, but also dissatisfied with myself. I described my ideal weight as 100 pounds. At first, I described my appearance as "too thin," but I crossed it out and instead circled "okay." I admitted my fear of becoming obese. I described my diet as avoiding red meat, bread, most dairy products, and desserts.

Typical of people with eating disorders, I admitted my preference of eating alone. One theory for this is that coexisting with anorexia is social phobia and paranoia about being watched while eating, or eating in public.

I also admitted to binge eating once a week, usually on the day before I was weighed at the doctor's office. On binges I ate cake, pie, pastries, cookies, chocolates and candies, ice cream and dairy products, tea, coffee or water, fruit, vegetables, popcorn, or cereal. I'd consume 10 cookies, a dozen chocolates, three dishes of ice cream, lots of vegetables, large bowls of popcorn or cereal, or a container of strawberries, over a period of two to three hours. The greater the stress, anxiety, and guilt I felt, the more likely I was to binge eat. I felt anxiety, anger, guilt, and depression before bingeing, although at the time I wasn't able to identify my emotions. I admitted to bingeing alone and feeling self-critical and exhausted afterwards. I sometimes was confused about whether or not I was hungry; however, at other times I felt intense hunger. I recognized hunger but denied it, believing that I had extraordinary self-discipline.

Circumstances that triggered binge eating included realizing that I had consumed very few calories all day. I knew that the number of calories I had eaten did not sustain life, and deep down inside I wanted to live. Some research states that people with anorexia nervosa are not hungry. If that is true, it often wasn't the case with me. I often felt very, very hungry. The dysfunctional habit of eating basically nothing during the day and bingeing at night started with the camping trip I took with my aunt years before. Since this practice "worked" for my skinny aunt and provided a "high" from low blood sugar, I adopted it and it became a lifestyle. I had no idea how hard it would be to change it. It is called night-eating syndrome and there are few effective ways to overcome it. One is to eat breakfast regularly and establish a structured method of spacing adequate and nutritious caloric intake throughout the day. When done for an extended time until new habits are formed, a person can overcome this habit.

I fasted for 24 to 48 hours at a time, at least once a week. I did not use laxatives or diuretics. I used appetite suppressants called AYDS chocolates. When mom used to buy them for herself, I'd steal some from her bedroom. AYDS were appetite suppressant candy with benzocaine to numb the mouth and phenylpropanolamine, which is in the same family as amphetamines (speed).

The questionnaire had a section to write a description of myself and I wrote:

> *Quite mixed-up and unsure of myself. I'm not the person I would like to be. I'm eager to be out of school and this town. I'm not happy in school, and it shows. I try to be happy at home, but it's usually forced. I want help with my eating habits and to be normal. I'm upsetting to my family and this makes me feel guilty. I have high expectations of myself: university, living on my own, being able to take care of myself. I'm annoyed because I know that I am unable to do that now, and*

scared as well. I feel like this is my last chance to get my act together to beat this bloody sickness; I'm sick and tired of it. I'm worried about missing schoolwork and failing grade 12. I'm not interested in the opposite sex, and I know I should be. I'm not interested in partying, and I know I should be. I have a dreadful fear of fat. I enjoy the high feeling that I get from exercising.

I described my dad as "very hard-working." I wrote:

> He is strong, gentle, patient, very devoted, loving, kind, and determined. I get along with him very well. Lately it's been better than ever because I know he loves me a lot, even more than our farm and his cows.

I always felt like I was lower priority than the farm, crops, and cows. I felt guilty because I was a burden. I felt guilty when dad would stop what he was doing, like bringing pails of fresh milk to the house, to throw the softball and play catch with me for a few minutes. I complained when I had to do farm work, like hauling bales. I wanted and treasured any attention, even a glance, from my dad. I thought that being sick might give me more attention from him, but instead he seemed to retreat further from me. He probably felt helpless.

I described my mom as "beautiful inside and out." I wrote:

> She is my best friend. We know each other very well and can always read each other's feelings. I love her so much. She is the best, closest person in the world to me. She has many friends and loves life.

When describing my social life, I stated:

I have not gone out with anyone for a while. I am afraid of older men because of past relationships. I don't go out very much lately because I have no real desire to and no one to go out with.

I described myself as moody, edgy and unhappy at school. I admitted to being anxious, nervous and tense most of the time, especially when faced with a new situation.

I described my exercise habits as daily and compulsive. Jogging and running had recently changed to walking. Mom said it was because I was too weak to run, but I didn't recognize any weakness. I would also skip rope, do aerobic exercises and sit-ups, and whatever else I could think of. I tried to convince myself that my motivation was to improve cardiovascular fitness and muscle tone, and for enjoyment. But I actually did it to burn calories, work out muscle stiffness, and because I felt I had to in order to feel good about myself. I exercised because it would make me so tired that I would just go to bed and forget everything. I exercised because I was alone and bored and didn't know what else to do. I exercised because I liked the high I got from it, and because I didn't think I could stop, and most of the time I didn't want to.

I described the precipitating events to my eating disorder as:

When I was 15, I thought I had been raped and was pregnant. Before that, I was always exposed to and trying diets. I'd go on my own 1,000-calorie-a-day diets, and then 800 calories, and less and less. My sister graduated high school and left home. I felt neglected. I was left to take care of myself while alone at home. I lost my steady boyfriend and my best friend. I wanted to be the best in sports and schoolwork and everything and was always pushing myself so I could break the limits and see what I can handle. I'm damn sick and tired of it and I want help.

Responses to the *Eating Attitudes Test* showed classic anorexia behavior patterns. I often prepared food for others but did not eat what I cooked. I always got anxious before eating and was terrified about being overweight. I often avoided eating when I was hungry, because I was afraid I would lose control and eat fattening foods or too much food. I was preoccupied with food. I always cut my food into small pieces because I read somewhere that I could fool myself into thinking I was eating more food because that made it look like more. I used small plates because I read that it tricks the brain into thinking there is more food. I often used chopsticks because it takes longer to eat that way. I often ate the same foods day after day because then I didn't need to worry that I was eating so much that I would get fat, because I didn't get fat the day before. I intentionally took a long time to eat meals because I heard that it takes the brain 20 minutes to tell the stomach that it's full. I drank very hot liquids with meals to burn my mouth so I couldn't taste the food and that might make me eat less. The battle in my own mind was unrelenting.

I admitted to weighing myself several times a day. I liked all clothing to fit loosely at this point, contrary to early in the disease when I prided myself on being thin and wore tight-fitting clothes that emphasized my body.

The *Eating Disorders Inventory (EDI)* revealed many classic anorectic thought processes. I was torn between the desire to remain a child, and the desire to become an adult. I sometimes wished I could be younger and return to the security of childhood; however, at the same time I wanted to be an adult. I wanted the torturous teenage years stuck in between childhood and adulthood to end.

I was often confused about what emotion I was feeling. I felt emotionally empty inside, or experienced feelings that I could not identify. Because of the insatiable quest for self-control, I worried that my feelings would get out of control. Because of this, I had trouble expressing my emotions to other people. Close relationships were rare. I wanted to keep people at a certain distance and felt uncomfortable if they got too close. I rarely trusted others and often felt alone in the world. I also believed that only outstanding performance was acceptable and hated being less than best at things. I usually tried very hard to avoid disappointing my parents and teachers. Low self-esteem is a monster just under the surface of anorexia. I often felt inadequate or ineffective, and wished I were someone else. I usually set very high standards for myself and felt that I must do things perfectly, or not do them at all.

The *Eating Disorder Inventory Profile* compared my pretreatment EDI subscale scores with those of an average female college student. The "Drive for Thinness" score was over three times that of the average female college student. The "Bulimia" score was also four times greater. Although I hadn't used vomiting as a method of weight management, I was desperate and likely would have if I had thought about it. I felt additional pressure when I knew others who didn't know me were watching me. I felt extreme guilt knowing that my mom was anxious, ashamed, and angry when others saw my odd habits. I knew she would rationalize my behavior later when I left the room. My "body dissatisfaction" score was half that of the average college female. This is not surprising to me because most of the time I was very proud of how I looked, even at my lowest weight. I was vain and prideful with the knowledge that while many were struggling with carrying too much weight, I was not. While many would eat beyond the number of calories needed to sustain life, I knew I could still exist on a lot less. My clothing was not tight, and when I looked at my naked body in the mirror I was satisfied with my profile. I believed that I had self-discipline beyond anyone else and it showed in my appearance. I did not know that I had lost control to the disease at that point.

Vanity, self-love, and conceit are drivers in the development and maintenance of anorexia. My "interpersonal distrust" score was three times higher than that of the average female college student (likely a downstream effect of the rape). "Introceptive awareness" was extremely above average at nearly ten times that of the average female college student. I surmise that this score is the result of meeting with the locum doctors in town for over a year, having many discussions with my mother about anorexia, and the seminar that I attended in the city where I learned about the eating disorders program at City Hospital. I also knew what to say and what people wanted to hear. I knew all about anorexia and used it to manipulate anyone who thought they could help or cure me. I felt empowered with knowledge about the disease, but ironically, unable to rein it in. It's like a person who knows and quotes scripture straight from the Bible, but does not, cannot, or chooses not to practice its principles in their own life.

Why do you call me, "Lord, Lord," and do not do what I say?

Luke 6:46

I obtained copies of most of my medical records from the hospital stay. Medical records provide insight into many of the physical and psychological aspects of anorexia nervosa. It's important for a person with anorexia to understand the damage they are doing to their own mind and body.

Gaining Insight

Physician notes:

History of presenting illness: Dates back to July 1984 during the early summer months. The origin of the problem appears to be twofold. Around this time, the patient was allegedly at a party, where she and a 26-year-old man drank too much alcohol and passed out together. She woke up very worried that she had intercourse with this fellow, and that she may be pregnant. As well, in the summer of 1984 her older sister was graduating from high school and this was her only sibling. Apparently, her older sister received a great deal of attention from both of her parents as this was the first family graduation. As well, her sister was attractive, academically and physically talented, and Adrienne felt a lot of competition and some resentment for her sister because of this. Before the summer of 1984, Adrienne participated in diets that her mother and sister were taking part in just to feel that she belonged. She lost 20 to 25 pounds before the school year started. When she started school in September things got even worse, as she had become amenorrheic and she was very worried that she might perhaps be pregnant because of this incident earlier on in the summer. The situation lightened a bit in early November 1984 when she got a light menses, and this was her last menstrual period.

In November 1984 she was encouraged by her parents to attend their small-town general physician, after she told her parents of the alleged rape and they noticed her marked weight loss. She was seen initially every two weeks for counseling, which resulted in no real change in her eating behavior. During this time the patient would eat mainly vegetarian and fruit diet with little or no meat products. She engaged in multiple long exercise activities including marathons, sprinting and biking. She denied several times the use of laxatives, diuretics, diet pills, or emesis. She admitted to occasional binge eating, followed by somnolence one to two episodes per week. She was admitted for anorexia for several days in November 1984 and discharged for reasons of school attendance. She was hospitalized again in January 1985 for several weeks, at the request of the local doctor and her parents. At this time, she weighed 74 pounds. She was given whatever she wanted to eat in the hospital and was not forced to engage in any self-monitoring behaviors.

Since this discharge from hospital, she has been seeing the GP approximately once a week for a one-hour counseling session. She feels that no real changes resulted in her behaviors as a result of counseling, and her weight is fairly stable in the 81-86 pound range from month to month. She considers her ideal body weight to be 99 to 100 pounds at 5 feet 4 inches tall.

Past history: This patient has no past significant medical history. She was diagnosed as having Raynaud's Syndrome for two years, with no major complications. She did not have any of the childhood diseases. She has no previous significant psychiatric history, though she does admit to having labile moods. She has only had suicidal ideation once, but never in the last 18 months. She suffered a syncopal episode in summer of 1984 from too much sun, and a CT scan of the head was performed which was normal. Gynecologic history: the patient had menarche at age 13 with menstrual periods every 5 to 6 weeks, lasting 3 days. She has had amenorrhea since November 1984. She denies any pregnancies in the past.

Consultant notes:

History: 17-year-old female living with parents. Anorexia, depression.

Normal weight, normal eating until summer 1984. Spent the

night with an older man, too drunk to remember details, and in the morning, thought she had been raped.

After this started restricting her intake drastically, mainly eating vegetables and fruit, little protein. No shoplifting. Weight has decreased gradually. Body image — does not feel thin. Exercising is excessive. Involved in every sport possible at school, walks about three hours on weekend days and about 3 miles on weekdays as well. No vomiting. No laxatives.

Frequent depression: felt suicidal last year and spent a lot of time in cold weather to hurt self. Strong family history of depression.

Patient History: No major illness except anorexia and Raynaud's disease. No allergies except peanut butter. Product of normal pregnancies, no infant feeding troubles. Psych admission 2x this year for anorexia.

Family History: Paternal grandmother depressed, in and out of hospital and gets depressed each winter. Treated with antidepressants. Aunts x 2 with depression. No ETOH or other psychiatric illness. Thyroid disease: paternal aunt

Social: Sister 20 years old. Nursing student at University. Mom is a CNA, dad is a farmer.

Self: High school student, "A" student. Few friends now; "too moody." No boyfriend (but has in past). Pretty girl, ++ thin, eye contact good. Looks anxious, slightly sad looking, feels sad. Sleep normal. Appetite okay but wants to be thin. Gets high from fasting. Not suicidal. Thought formation normal. Thought content: Some obsessional traits regarding worrying about school, family members, etc. Demanding of self.

Cognitive: Claims that her concentration is poor but there is no evidence of such today. Memory is good. Insight seems good. Understanding seems good, seems a very intelligent girl.

Summary: 17-year-old female with 2-year history of anorexia with some bingeing. Anorexia started after a traumatic event. A high achieving, bright girl.

Vital signs: Temperature: 35.7 degrees Celsius (96.26 degrees Fahrenheit). Pulse: 44 bpm, weak. BP: 104/90. Respirations: 16. Height: 63 ¼ cm. Weight: 36.9 kilograms (81.35 pounds). HN: Pupils equal and reactive with normal fundi but not visualized well. Pharynx normal, no adenopathy, Thyroid normal.

Respirations clear. Cardiovascular: S1 S2 normal. No bruits. Peripheral pulses weak but all palpable. Femoral pulses strong. Hands cyanotic, slow refilling, toes cyanotic. Abdomen: Thin with no masses, no organomegaly, bowel sounds normal. Extremities: thin ++ muscle bulk decreased, tone normal, reflexes symmetrical.

Summary: 17-year-old female with anorexia and Raynaud disease. Plan: Admit, assess, increase weight.

Admission note:

January 2, 1987

Weight 84.5 pounds. Weighed 74 pounds in January 1986. Was in the hospital for 6 weeks. Highest weight in past few years was 89 pounds. Anorexia X 2 years. Attends grade 12. 17 years old.

Eats salads, vegetables, cereals.

Gaining Insight

Menses stopped 2 years ago. Weighed 110 before anorexia and thought she was fat. Height is 5 feet 4 inches.

Has one sister — 20 years old. Takes nursing at university. No brother. Father is 48 and a farmer. Mother is 42 and a CNA.

Patient thought "I should do something about anorexia." Patient wants to attend clinic and group therapy. She heard us speak at the general public meeting.

Academics are okay — 72% average. No special problems. A teacher told her sister that the patient's concentration is not so good. Patient plans to attend university.

January 13, 1987

Letter from Dr. Thomas to locum physician:

Date seen — December 23, 1986

Thank you for referring Adrienne. This 17-year-old anorexic girl is now inpatient in the psychiatric unit of the hospital. She is 5 feet four inches tall. Her symptoms were low weight (84 pounds), anuria of two years, distorted body image, hyperactivity, manipulative behavior regarding her food intake, depression, bradycardia (pulse 40 per minute), poor peripheral circulation, and denial of her illness.

Adrienne is cooperating with the treatment program which is as follows:

- Complete bedrest.

- Voluntary restriction in cutting down verbal communications, not to read or entertain herself in any way.

- Diet counseling.

- Medical supervision regarding her electrolytes and cardiac condition, etc.

- Control of anorexic symptoms with hypnosis.

- Psychodrama to increase her total awareness.

Adrienne is now responding to the treatment regime in the hospital. Her mood has improved, she is gaining weight and her peripheral circulation has made tremendous recovery.

Thank you for allowing Adrienne to come to our facility for treatment of her anorexia nervosa.

With personal best regards,

Dr. Thomas, F.R.C.P. (C)

Apply your heart to instruction and your ears to words of knowledge.

Proverbs 23:12 (NIV)

Seeing a Vision

Sometime after agreeing to the intensive treatment program, I was lying in bed in the middle of the morning, thinking and praying. The door to my private hospital room was kept open all of the time. A plain armchair sat in the way so the door could not close unless the chair was moved. I felt the presence of God in the room with me. When I looked over at the chair, Jesus was sitting in it. He had long brown hair, a moustache and a short beard. He had a look of peace on his face. He was wearing the typical blue and white robe and sandals that he wears in children's Sunday school books. His hands were clasped together loosely on his lap. God revealed himself to me in the person of Jesus, and He was sitting in my hospital room! I could not look away. Jesus did not look up at me. He just sat there looking down. The message I received from the vision of Jesus was that this was *right*. It was all part of His plan. I was in the right place now and I would be taken care of. I knew He was guarding the door. He did not stay there for a long time, it might have been minutes, but the feeling of peace remained with me every day thereafter. I was hesitant to tell anyone about this vision because of what they might think. You know, people who see things that are not really there are "crazy." Well, call me crazy, but Jesus was sitting in a chair in my hospital room, and He gave me peace beyond understanding.

Whoever acknowledges me before others, I will also acknowledge before my Father in heaven.

Matthew 10:32 NIV

Guilt

Finally getting enough food and fluids to clear the fog in my brain, I tried to make sense of past events. This is a dream I had while in the hospital. It was frighteningly true to life. Back home on the farm, tension was thick in the air most of the time. It was especially tense at mealtimes or when there was anything happening that involved food. I think that's where this dream came from.

> I dreamed that I was back at home. It was Christmas and my relatives were at our house. I had just woken up and looked at the clock. It was 10:00 a.m. As usual, my first thought was "it is too late for breakfast, wait for lunch" although I was hungry. Dad and my uncle were sitting at one end of the table. My sister was having breakfast. She asked my mom to make her another piece of toast and she was eating it. My cousin Shirley was eating toast. They all watched me as I came into the kitchen, but nobody said anything. I knew they were waiting for me to make myself some breakfast. I got that old, sick, scared feeling back. I ignored them and looked in first one, and then the other Tupperware containers on the table for bread. There were two half-crusts of bread left. I put them in the toaster and right away they started burning because they were too small. I ignored it because I liked toast burnt black because it would be small, hard, dried out, and taste bad. So I left it burning and stalled, hoping it would burn more, and I went to the bathroom. I knew if I stayed there, Mom would

give me heck for burning my toast. When I came out, I saw Mom grab the burnt toast and throw them down. "Why can't you ever eat anything I make?" she said loudly. "Isn't it good enough for you?" She handed me this big plate of toast she had already made that I honestly hadn't seen before. It was buttered, so I didn't want it. Then I saw Mom. She was upset. Her face was red and she was crying. She was embarrassed because of everyone watching and listening to us. She slammed the Cheez Whiz jar on the table and walked away. I got that old lump in my throat and felt ashamed and guilty for hurting her, again. So I took two small pieces of toast and walked past my aunt and cousin sitting on the couch and went to my room. I was crying. I went back out to the living room and asked my aunt if she wanted to come talk to me. She followed me to my room, and then I woke up, still crying.

Let us draw near to God with a sincere heart and with the full assurance that faith brings, having our hearts sprinkled to cleanse us from a guilty conscience and having our bodies washed with pure water.

Hebrews 10:22

Guilt had been overwhelming me for years. While hospitalized, I finally could release it onto paper. Much of the journaling I did came from a place of regret and shame. I felt like I had destroyed my family and wounded my friends. This is some of what I journaled.

I remember for my birthday last year, Mom asked me what I would like for a special supper, because she always made us whatever we wanted on our birthdays. I said Chinese food. She made rice, eggrolls, fish, shrimp, everything I like, fortune

Guilt

cookies, too. And vanilla ice cream. We had my godmother over too because it was also her birthday. I had no close friends from school that I either wanted to come or would have wanted to come out to the farm.

(Just two years earlier, before I got sick, I would have several friends come out to the farm and spend the night at our place and we would have a very loud, active, fun time.)

Mom made all of this stuff for me, and a cake too. No one else was crazy about this food, but she made it for me anyways. I said there was a good TV program on and asked if I could go watch it instead of sitting at the table. Mom said I could, but I knew she didn't really want me to because we had company and it was rude, but she let me go anyways and didn't say anything. Well, I filled up my plate and made it look really good and I went into the living room with it. I then made a couple of trips back and forth to my room, getting napkins and paper towels to wrap the food up in and throw it into the garbage. I threw almost all of it away. Mom asked me how I liked it and I said, "Really good," and I think Mom was happy. I feel bad about that. I wonder if she knew. Mom has always bought me everything I wanted, from granola to shrimp, crab, special cereals, chips, lentils, legumes, breads, muffins, and desserts. That stuff is expensive. I wish there was some way to let her know that I appreciated all of those things. Once when I told her she said "That's what a mother is for." She loves me, so that's why she did it. I love her, and Dad too. He was always the strong one. He has really given me strength to be here in the hospital. I've never seen my dad cry. He's too strong. But I think he was almost crying when he dropped me off here. I don't know how much more I can write right now, but this is only part. I have a lot more I could write. One day I'm going to write a book, I think.

I wrote more in a school essay called the "Summer Chapter." It is about what happened last summer. Every word that I wrote is the truth. I may not be able to speak about my thoughts and feelings, but I can write them. The only people who have read the essay are my English teacher and my sister. It feels so good to get it all out. It's such a relief that I could go to sleep right now because I feel so much better.

> I lie down and sleep; I wake again,
> because the Lord sustains me.
>
> Psalm 3:5 (NIV)

This is the essay I wrote after two years of living with anorexia nervosa. I called it The Summer Chapter.

> I shall start first by saying that I hope to make this essay a chapter of a book sometime in the future. This book will describe my life from when I was born, until that present day, but focus mainly on a specific portion: the time when I turned 15 years old until I graduate from high school at the age of 18. Because I don't want this essay to turn into a book in itself, I will just write about this past summer, the summer of 1986.
>
> This summer I was allowed to work away from home at a summer resort. I applied for a job there the year before and knew that my chance of getting one was good because Catherine had worked there for three years, and she was popular and people liked her. My parents were very eager to let me do whatever made me happy, and they often told me that. But there were certain things that had to become realities before I could go and work on my own. It was the same old deal. I had to be 90 pounds to be able to go. It was a requirement set by my parents and my doctor. They said it was for my own good because any weight less than 90 pounds would leave me too weak to work. They underestimated the power of the human

Guilt

body when it's pushed to its limits.

I was to start work on June 27. If I recall correctly, the week before that I put on three pounds. That was a gigantic, tremendous amount for me to put on in a week, but I wanted to go, bad. So I did it. It was not put on in a healthy way. Some day (in my book) I will explain some characteristics and behavior patterns of my disease — anorexia nervosa.

I had a doctor's appointment on June 26. When I stepped on the scale and I was 88 pounds, my doctor and parents were happy, but suspicious. They voiced their suspicions, but I reassured them that everything was all right. I can be very persuasive when I want to be. In fact, I had them convinced to let me go before I reached my goal of 90 pounds. The next day, Mom and I went to the resort. I was there getting a haircut when I got a call to start work immediately. I was in a panic but tried not to show it as we rushed through my haircut and ran to work. I started work at a fast-food place (ironically) cooking and serving burgers, fries, pizza (all forbidden foods for me), and ice cream.

The next few days went by in a blur. The drive-in was very busy because it was the holiday weekend. I was very tired but would never admit it. I was run down and weak because I was eating next to nothing. I was so happy to be away from the pressure at home at mealtimes that I felt like a bird let out of a cage. It didn't matter to me what people thought of me when I worked extra hours, would not eat anything at work, and took off for hour-long runs in the mornings. I just did not care. I knew that the people I worked with knew something was wrong with me but didn't know what or what to do about it. My physical appearance, moodiness, and strange actions (like hiding out by myself in my room) probably frightened them. Although my coworkers were my age, I never really got to be friends with them.

I lived in a place called "rez" (workers residence) which was an old two-story building. The ground floor was a bar. I had one roommate. She began bringing guys into our room at night and would go at it in the bed two feet away from me. The noises made me nauseous. I could not handle it anymore, and as soon as the chance arose, I moved out. I had lots of stuff to move, and the only empty room left to move into was one with three beds, holes in the walls, and had never been cleaned. I cleaned, dusted, washed walls, scrubbed floors, etc., so that I could move in. (That is another characteristic of my illness, compulsive cleaning). I was dating a guy who lived just down the hall from me. I liked him because he made me feel special. Besides his good looks, he had a good sense of humor and made me laugh, which at that time was very rare. I found out he was 28 years old. I should have had more brains then to get mixed up with a man who was eleven years older than me, but I was flattered that an older man was actually paying attention to me.

But then it got scary. He was a drug dealer and did a lot of drugs himself. He worked at the family mortuary so likely was used to seeing corpses. That's probably why my physical appearance didn't bother him. He never pressured me to do drugs; that wasn't the problem. He would smoke them, or shoot them, or whatever, and come visit me in the middle of the night. I didn't know what to do. I felt very vulnerable but craved the affection and attention of a man (any man). I was literally starving for affection. Even though I hadn't had a period for months and knew it was unlikely that I would get pregnant, we did a lot but didn't have intercourse. I thank God for that because the situation could have been a lot worse. People had warned me about what a "womanizer" he was but, of course, I thought I knew better and I ignored them. They were not stupid. They were right about him. I eventually told

Guilt

Thank you for providing a way for me to write this story.

English teacher's comments:

There is not much possible in response to such a well-organized and written composition. Just the ability to write on this is much more important than how it was written. You now see why the emotional aspect is so much stronger in a composition with personal qualities. If we all wrote more often about ourselves, the various problems faced would seem easier to deal with!

My English teacher inspired me to journal, write essays, and put my thoughts and feelings into words. If I had stuffed all of that inside me for the anorexia years, I would not have made it through. She encouraged me to write, even at the depths of anorexia when I felt hopeless and helpless.

Therefore confess your sins to each other and pray
for each other so that you may be healed. The prayer
of a righteous person is powerful and effective.

James 5:16 (NIV)

Journaling: school

I'd like to talk about what it has been like in school over the last two years. Over the summer when I lost all that weight, I broke up with my boyfriend. We were going steady for about a year and a half. When I think back now, it seems so minor; it doesn't bug me now, but it did for a while when it happened. After I got back to school, I was 20 pounds lighter.

No one had seen me over the summer, so I looked different

to everyone, and everyone looked differently at me. Some kids asked me if I had cancer. Another kid asked if I had AIDS. I was given the nickname "Rocky" because I ran cross-country at noon and after school. I was stubborn and would give it all I had. My gym teacher, Mr. Mike, would urge me on, and I ran through blisters, aching muscles and joints, and scary episodes of chest pain. He seemed to recognize that if I was determined enough, I could beat everyone. I was headstrong and wanted to be better than all the other girls, and even boys. I had more endurance than the girls, and I kept up with most of the boys. It felt good to be able to do that, and I was so proud. I never told anyone, and I tried not to be boastful, but inside I felt a real sense of accomplishment. I was good at something. I'd leave my lunch at noon, telling myself that I'd eat it after practice, but, of course, who would feel like eating right after running? It was just an excuse. Boys at school started calling me "Skinny," and I would feel proud. I weighed around 90 pounds. I would wear tight clothes that showed off my hip bones. At first, my best friend, Sarah, tried to compete with me. I knew what she was doing. She started race-walking at home, lifting weights, and would wear low-cut shirts to school and point out her chest cavity bones to me in the mirror in the girls' bathroom. She was so proud to have lost about five pounds. She would weigh herself daily and had a big colorful exercise calendar on her wall at home, which she would show me. I would look, and then go home and do more. I thought, "I'll lose more." "I'll be better."

It was the same way with my sister. We used to do exercise records together, side-by-side. I was always trying to do more, to be better. Those songs still haunt me. I know all the words and where the records skipped. When Catherine would jog down the lane at night, I would jog down the pasture lane. It was shorter, but I would either run instead of jogging, or go farther and farther. Mom and Dad urged me to have a milkshake after a run, but no way would I ever do that. Catherine and I would eat supper at 5:30. I would eat mainly the same thing that she would, but when I looked at her at a normal weight, and I'd see her eating cinnamon buns or something, I wouldn't. I wanted to be "better." The competition in my mind continued until Catherine moved out and went to college. I was 15. I knew even then that she was not competing with me, just me with her, like I did with almost everyone. Before anorexia, Catherine and I had so many fun times, playing games and doing things together on the farm. At school we got along well, and I was always "little sister" to her friends and people her age. I felt special and really liked that. After she left, the only person left to compete with was myself, and I didn't feel so special anymore.

My mom would pack lunch for me to take to school and I would not eat it. It was always perfectly made, specially prepared, and whatever I wanted. I started by throwing only part of it away, and then I'd throw more away or feed it to the dog as I was leaving our yard in the morning. Mom probably knew this. I also went from walking to running nearly a mile to meet the bus, and from walking home after school to running home. I usually had a whole knapsack full of books on my back. They were so heavy sometimes I could have cried, but I was too stubborn to cry. In fact, I added books to make it heavier. I'd run up and down those hills with my heavy knapsack to catch the bus. I could have walked. The damn bus would have waited, but no. That's how I developed bruises, and then sores over the bones of my back. They went from being red, raw, and bleeding to partially healing, and then they'd open up again.

I found it painful to sit because my pelvic bones rubbed against my jeans, so I usually wore sweatpants. Mom would be so worried, and it looked like she would start crying when she saw them. She would tenderly put Band-Aids on them. Just recently she saw them and all she said was, "Oh God." That's all. I didn't know what to say, so I said "thank you" when she was done bandaging. After that, she still never said anything and she wouldn't look at me, so I said, "I'm sorry, Mom." She burst out, "Don't say sorry, just do something!" Then we both cried separately, but we hugged later. I feel bad about that. Mom's nerves were bad sometimes, but it seemed that she learned to control them around other people.

My mom is strong, but when I cried, she would cry with me. We knew when one another was depressed or sad. When I lied and she found out, she'd say, "That's okay, I know it's not you lying; it's that damn disease." She tried to understand, and she'd hold me. I love her. I want to tell her about the lunches and thank her for all the love she put into them. They were so special, but I never ate even one whole lunch. If I didn't throw the lunch away before I got on the bus in the morning, I crumpled it up, not looking at it while on the bus, and threw it away at school. Or I left it in my lunch bag all day, crumpled, so I would not want it, or gave it away to someone at school. Sometimes I threw it away at the café that I walked to during a break from class, or took it home and put it back in the fridge. I'd drink water, or eat fruit, such as half of a kiwi or orange. I'd think, "I won't have a chance to walk it off this afternoon at school, no PE classes, so I won't eat, and then it will balance." I'd be restless and edgy in school all day because I had low blood sugar and I was starving.

At breakfast, I would pretend that I was eating and throw the food in our wood stove when I thought no one was looking. That has been done so many times, and the stove knows all of my burning secrets. I was just like a small child playing sick, stupid, little food games. I can't do it anymore. Lord help me to grow up. Lord help me.

Guilt

When I rode home on the bus and found no one there, I'd be happier than anything. I'd change into sweatpants, drink a quick Diet Coke or a little water, and go outside and run two and a half miles, often in bitter cold. By the time I was done, I was high from hunger and it felt great. It was hard to run, but I felt so good after. Or else I'd get the skipping rope that Mom had tried to hide from me and skip straight for up to one hour. I read somewhere that only top athletes can skip for that long. I was red and sweaty, had a stomachache, dizziness, and very sore ankles and feet. After about a week of skipping for an hour every day after school because it was too cold outside to run, my ankles felt like they were broken. I was limping and had to wear ankle braces. I told everyone it was from playing broom ball at school. I lied. Yet I kept on skipping, no matter how much it hurt, and when I couldn't for one or two days, I did floor exercises for an hour instead.

Whenever I was alone in the house, that's the first thing I thought of, whether it was 6 a.m. when Dad was outside and Mom was at work, or 4:30 p.m. when I got home, or 8 p.m. if Mom and Dad weren't home. I always refused to go to dinner or anywhere with them. I wanted to make my own food at home, that way I could have what I wanted. I'd also do it to see if I could choose healthy foods or if I could control myself when I was alone. I knew right from wrong when I prepared something to eat, but I'd block out all common sense. I'd make a big salad and drink very hot drinks. I'd put lemon pepper, vinegar, onion salt, garlic powder, chili pepper, or tabasco sauce on the food to kill my taste buds. It worked, but I'd feel hot and sick after eating. I always had to strain hard to go to the bathroom. I still do, and my heart pounds hard and fast. I don't think this is normal, and it scares me. I'd take about one hour to eat when I was alone and then I'd run around, doing dishes and cleaning. I had everything timed; I'd eat at 6 p.m. until 7 p.m., and then run around until 8 p.m. I would not sit down. Then I'd sit down at 8:00 and do homework in my room. This was also the way it was when school started in September and for months afterwards. This is called obsessive-compulsive disorder and often coincides with anorexia nervosa.

When Mom and Dad were home in the evening I was afraid of myself. Around 9 p.m. each night, they would make tea. To me that meant having something to eat to satisfy my stomach because it hurt. I felt out of control when I neared the fridge because I was so hungry. I'd try to think, "What should I have?" but it usually didn't work. Sometimes I'd start out with something not fattening, like a dish of plain cornflakes, and then I'd go back for more. I'd add other cereals, add vegetables, fruits, whatever. Sometimes I'd go to the fridge four or five times. I'd always walk by Mom and Dad. They knew I was struggling but they probably didn't know what to say or do, so they said and did nothing.

I would also have containers of frozen strawberries and they were so good. I'd eat lots of them, like maybe five cups. I'd make plain popcorn and eat massive bowls of it. Before Christmas, Mom bought candy and chocolates. I'd only have five per night, along with a bowl of plain cereal or popcorn or something. On the Saturday before I was admitted to the hospital, I felt so afraid. I was also hungry, and I had a large bag of popcorn with a half cup of chocolate chips and butterscotch chips melted in it. I was alone at home and my aunt and uncle were going to come home from the bar at about 12:30 a.m. I ate the popcorn for two hours.

I was so proud because I could control myself when I was alone. This is my greatest fear. My aunt and uncle arrived and I finished my popcorn. They were hungry and wanted to stay up and watch a movie. I saw my skinny aunty (who just had a baby) eating chocolate cookies. I thought, "If she can, so can I." I had one. I poured myself a bowl of plain cereal and sat down. She was still eating cookies. I went and poured the cereal back in the box. I got some chocolate Bridge Mix candy, peanut chocolate candy, and coconut chocolate candy, just a little of each. I savored them because I had denied myself all week. Then I remembered that I had a chocolate Cuban Lunch in my room. I ate that too. Aunty and Uncle seemed happy that I was eating. Dad came out of his bedroom and saw what I was eating. He smiled at me. I felt good but so full. I went to bed after having two more chocolate cookies. Aunty stayed up later. I was so full. After she went to bed, I couldn't sleep so I got up and ate 10 coconut candies and a bit of peanut brittle and a homemade chocolate. I don't know why. I was very nervous and tense, and I felt out of control, but not guilty. I just went to sleep. The next morning, I wasn't hungry, but I had strawberries (one bowl) for lunch and salad for supper. Well, that's it. That was my last binge, I hope. My very last. If I want it to be, I guess it will be.

    You wouldn't believe how much better you feel in the morning when you don't binge at night. I wouldn't eat all day until I was starving. Then I'd eat a lot. I'm sure my stomach could stretch like a cow belly if it had to. I was moody all day because of low blood sugar. I knew why, but other people didn't. They just thought I was moody. That's the main thing I'd like to get sorted out in my life, because I know that when I'm alone I just can't binge like that because it could grow into an obsession, or I could get real sick or something. I have to use self-control and try to eat enough during the day so I won't need to do that. Lord, help me. I think He will. I have more faith in Him now than I've ever had.

    I think He knows the time has come when I'm ready to accept His help. I am ready. It won't be that hard. I've made it this far, and now there's no turning back. I want to wear all *those nice clothes that I got for Christmas, like the new blue jeans. I tried them on this morning, and they are too big. My other jeans don't feel right either. They rub on my hip bones and the seams hurt. I can't wear them. My white pants feel too big on me. I hope that I will be able to learn to get used to my clothes when they fit better. My new vest falls off my shoulders, and I have no reason to wear a bra. It just gets in the way and you can see it because my shirt necks are too big. I can only wear loose sweatpants now because they don't hurt me. I think it's the same thing with a person who is too fat and can't wear their clothes; it's the same battle with yourself, day after day. It is exhausting.*

Come to me, all who are weary and
burdened, and I will give you rest.

Matthew 11:29 (NIV)

Journaling: grocery stores

I need to write about grocery stores. I wish I could figure out why I have a terrible fear of grocery stores. The only time I have no fear when I enter a grocery store is if I have no money at all. When I do though, I wander aimlessly, and the adrenaline in my brain speeds up and my heart races. It's not the same for clothes or jewelry or anything else. When I have to buy things in a grocery store, I can't decide what or how much to buy. I'm just like a small child. I want to get some things that I like, but I can't. I pick up things, put them back, empty bags, and fill bags. At least I've never stolen anything, so I don't need to feel guilty about that. I hope someday I'll be normal in a grocery store when I shop for myself... I have to be. I actually think that if I made a list of what I need and stuck exactly to it, I would be okay. I've tried that a couple of times and it mostly worked. I made my list at home before I went. For the past two years, I have always gone shopping with Mom or Dad. Just a couple of times I went alone.

    I'd like to talk about when I went up to the city to go Cristmas shopping in November. I went up on the long weekend. I will also tell you about my aunt and uncle. I rode up on the Greyhound bus by myself on Saturday morning. I've always gone shopping by myself for clothes and stuff for myself and other people. Anyway, I got there by 11 a.m. and put my stuff in a locker and went downtown to shop. I forget if I had a muffin for lunch, or just a Diet Coke. Then I shopped until 5:30 by myself, constantly, walking as fast as I could. Then I went to my aunt's place. She's 28 years old but looks about 16. She is a psych nurse. Apparently as a child she was very rebellious and was even in a cult once and almost killed. She moved out at 16 and got a job. She drinks a lot and does drugs. She is the aunt that I stayed with when I thought I was raped during the summer of 1984. Back then, we went on a trip, just me and her, up north to a lake.

    We pulled a trailer behind her car. We were at a party with people we didn't even know. I got talking to this guy who was about 30 years old. I was 15. He hit on me. I lied about my age and told him I was 17. I described my sister as myself and he believed me. We both drank too much. So did my aunt. It started to rain, and she took off in the car with a guy about 18 years old and went back to the trailer and left me. It was raining and this guy (Roy) told me to get in his tent, so I did. He zipped the tent closed. He had one sleeping bag. He crawled in and undressed — totally nude. It was the first time I had ever seen a nude man. He pulled me in and did up the sleeping bag. I sat up. I couldn't lie down. He tried to undress me, but I was crying and slapping his hands away. He asked me if I was a virgin and I said yes. He said that he didn't believe me. I was feeling sick and dizzy. Then I don't know what happened. When I woke up it had stopped raining. I was lying beside this totally nude guy in a sleeping bag. I was only partly dressed. I looked at my white sweatshirt and there were dark red stains on it like blood. I was terrified. Then Roy woke up. He sent me out to his car to get his underwear. His friends were still up partying. They saw me and made really rude comments and joked about my sweatshirt, saying it was blood because I had lost my virginity in the tent that night. I was scared and didn't know what I had done. He drove me back to our campsite where the trailer was parked and there, I open the door and see my aunt (who had just got engaged to a man back in the city) in bed with that 18-year-old. They got up in a hurry. Then Aunty asked me to change the sheets in the trailer. They were bloody. I felt nauseous but she made them breakfast. Then the guys left and so did we. I've told this story so many times. It has helped me to get it all out. Then I thought I was pregnant for five months until I got my period. I didn't tell anybody for five months after this happened.

 Back to when I went up to the city to shop. I had made an appointment for Monday to see a dietitian. I didn't tell anyone; I just did it. I felt like I wanted help. I took a cab and crosstown buses and got there by myself. The dietitian gave me a basic rule plan to follow, and a handbook and chart like they have here at City Hospital. She was really nice, and I did my best to follow her guide for about a week. After that, I found it really hard to follow, but when I was really in a panic, I'd look back at it and follow it. There's this one booklet called "Smart Snacking" that I've looked at a lot. It's helped me not to binge too much on junk. That's all I can write right now.

Guilt

For in my inner being I delight in God's law;
but I see another law at work in me, waging war
against the law of my mind and making me a
prisoner of the law of sin at work within me.

Romans 7:22-23 (NIV)

Journaling: my aunt

I always thought my aunt was "all that." She lives in the city, has long blonde hair, is thin, smokes like a chimney, and seems to live such a glamorous lifestyle. Aunty divorced several years earlier and has had many boyfriends since. Almost every time we go to visit or she visits us, she is with a different and often attractive man. There was no discipline when I stayed with her. Aunty stays up late smoking cigarettes and drinking alcohol, even when she was pregnant. She wakes up late and only drinks coffee all day until dinnertime, when she binge eats. I thought that was cool and followed the same dysfunctional eating plan when I stayed there with her. I just knew it was how she stayed so skinny, and I wanted to be just like her.

Aunty grows weed amongst the corn in the backyard. When I was about 13 and stayed there with her for a week during the summer, she gave me a small plastic baggie of marijuana seeds and told me to plant them out in the pasture near our farm and take care of them. She warned me not to tell Mom or Dad or even my sister. When I got home, I hid the baggie by taping it to the back of my mirror on the dresser in my bedroom. I remember going out to the pasture and finding a place to plant them but not doing it. I think I was worried that it wouldn't be a good enough place; there wasn't enough water, it wasn't hidden enough, or I wouldn't be able to find it later. I don't remember what ultimately happened, but the seeds never got planted. Somehow Mom found out, but I didn't get in trouble. I just remember feeling so guilty.

My aunt always had tasks for my dad to do. She had boyfriends but used my dad to do things like fix her sliding glass closet door. He had a farm to manage all by himself, and a two-hour drive to get to her place, but he usually did it anyway. Once, my dad went to visit her. When she was not home, he thought he would "weed" the garden for her, and he pulled up all of her marijuana plants and threw them away. He was just trying to help. Apparently, she was really upset about that. When I went to my aunt's house by myself, there was always alcohol and often marijuana cookies free for the taking in the freezer downstairs. I would help myself to all of it. She took me to a house party with her once when I was about 15 years old. There was no one there even near my age, so I walked around all of the older people, feeling alone in a house packed with people. The smell of pot plus alcohol was strong, and I felt lonely but very mature. When I walked into the kitchen, there were people standing around the stove holding spoons. They were melting something in the spoons. I asked someone what it was and was told it was black hash. Even though I was still confused I knew it was drugs, and I was terrified. I left the kitchen as fast as I could and did not see anyone ingest or inject it. I can still see that in my mind.

After I went on the camping trip with my aunt and was sexually abused. I told my mom, she told my dad. Mom told me later that he drove two hours to confront my aunt. She told my dad that what happened to me at that party was not her fault. She told him that I should have been responsible for *myself. A 15-year-old drinking alcohol, at a party with strangers, who is left overnight should be responsible for herself? Of course, when I heard that she said that, the familiar feelings of guilt and shame filled me. "I should have stayed right beside my aunt. I shouldn't have jumped into the lake with the other people. I should have stayed by the car the whole time. I should not have drunk the alcohol they gave me. I should have fought harder after I was pushed in the tent.*

> Flee from sexual immorality. All other sins a person commits are outside the body, but whoever sins sexually, sins against their own body.
>
> 1 Corinthians 6:18 (NIV)

Journaling: Carson Hospital

This is what I can remember doing in Carson Hospital. I went in in January of 1986. I was in for six weeks. I think I went in on the 15th. When I went in, I was in a single room. I thought of it as an outing, but I was quite scared to be taken from home. My mom is a CNA and had all her shifts changed to nights while I was there, because we thought it would be better that way. When I went in, I took everything I wanted. I took dolls, special blankets, stuffed animals, lots of clothes, everything. I had my own TV, radio, alarm clock, throw mats, etc. I even hauled a rocking chair into my room and covered it with blankets. I had it neat and tidy, and all set up exactly how I wanted it. I even got to choose between three rooms and select the one I liked best. I put up posters and calendars. I had my own private bathroom and got to shower and bath whenever I wanted, and even have whirlpool baths.

Where should I begin? With the exercise, I guess. I put down the thickest mats in the bathroom, in front of the mirror, so that I could jog and run and jump on them and I wouldn't be heard out in the hall or downstairs. I remember exactly where the floor creaks when you jump on it, and I would not step there. I tried to keep my door closed at all times so people could not see me do sit-ups on my bed or stretches and splits on the floor. I exercised every chance I got when no one was looking. I would stay in the bathroom for up to a half-hour at a time, just running and counting jumps. I always had the radio on in my room outside the bathroom door so that I could listen to it and run to the music and hear the time. I would get all flushed and breathing hard and tired and worn out. I would get a "high" feeling. Sometimes nurses would come and knock on the door. "Are you exercising, Adrienne?" they would ask. "Oh, no," I would reply and flush the toilet or run water in the sink. My legs constantly ached and my feet had callouses. I knew the routine of the hospital so that whenever they went downstairs for coffee I could exercise more, and I could hear them come up again, and I'd stop. I knew when they had to go to the desk, when they were down the hall, the sound of their shoes in the hall. When the nurses and doctors found out, I had to keep the door open. That was no problem to me. I exercised more in the bathroom, or behind the door, or behind the bed.

When I took a bath in my tub, I would move around, splash, scrub the tub, the floor, the walls, and dirty every towel just so I could get clean ones from down the hallway. I would scrub the sink as well. When I'd shower, I'd go early in the morning at 6:30 a.m., when I knew the nurses were busy. I'd take loads of towels. I would turn the water on very hot because I'd read that steam burns off calories, and I'd fluctuate the temperature so that I would have to keep moving and burn calories to stay warm. I'd be in there for ages, and when I was done and could not take anymore (I was so tired), I would clean the entire bathroom with spray disinfectant, scrub the floors and walls on my hands and knees, and then scrub the room down, quickly, because the nurses would be telling me to hurry up. After that I would change towels.

I was able to use the whirlpool about four times when I was in the hospital. I would swim in it for 30 to 45 minutes. The nurses would come in once or twice but leave right away and I was mostly on my own. The water would be on as hot as it went. I'd fill it with bubbles and put the water on full blast. The nurses would tell me to get out after about 30 minutes, so I would empty it, scrub the floor, the walls, the tub, the sink, around the toilet, and everywhere I could see. I would make messes so I could clean them up. Then I would go back to my room.

It didn't take long before the staff suspected what I was doing, and the doctor prescribed Valium and these other relaxants that you put under your tongue. They left the ones that go under your tongue in my room because I asked them to. I took them after I was done exercising, or I threw them away. I always told the doctor and nurses that they only helped a little. The nurses would ask me if I wanted Valium, but I was terrified that it would work, so I never said yes. They gave me one at meals and I would either throw it away or take it and then exercise before it would take effect, and even keep going after. I would be so dizzy though.

I also asked to go outside for walks. They let me walk around the hospital by myself or with a nurse. With a nurse I could go further, so I usually went with one. It was the middle of winter, but I still insisted.

Every morning at 11, I would see Dr. Erickson. At first, I was terrified of him, but then he became like my best friend.

In his office, I would cry because I was tired and hungry, but I wouldn't tell him that. He would tell me to write down my feelings and I did, but I left out all the games and tricks I was playing on myself. I drew a picture of this devil. Dr. Erickson convinced me to talk about many incidents that I otherwise would not have. I was closer to him than my father, and I always told him, "When you leave, I'm going too." He left at the end of February, and he let me go too. He was a "locum," which essentially means a temporary doctor filling in when there are no other doctors.

I went into the hospital at 74 lbs., and I came out at 76 lbs., I think.

I bought Dr. Erickson a stuffed animal and gave him Valentine's Day cards and chocolates before he left. That's how close I felt we were. I totally manipulated him, the poor guy. I wonder if he realizes that now.

I had to talk to nurses in the hospital about my diet. One was very overweight and probably didn't really care how she looked. She was not an inspiration to me at all. I made a pledge to myself to never be like her. "I like beef!" she would say. "I like pork chops, fried," she would say, "and big fried potatoes, and chocolate cake, yummy!" That really helped me (not). She gave me a food chart to fill out daily, but I would fill it out for the entire week. She said I had to have foods from the food groups, but I could pick them myself. I would feel that I had to deny myself the good foods, so I would either not write them down at all, or write them down and when they arrived, I would throw them down the sink or in the toilet. They got me everything I wanted. Mom would get muffins, tacos, whatever I asked for, from 100 miles away, and bring it home especially for me. What would I do with it? I would put it in a toaster oven that the nurses let me use and burn the hell out of it. I liked it that way, but then I would only eat part of it.

Guilt

No one watched me eat. I would eat alone. As soon as my tray came for every meal, the first thing I would do as soon as the nurses left my room was throw the milk down the sink. Then I would run back. Next, I would check everything over and compare it to my diet sheet, and check for errors. If there were errors, I would go get a nurse, demand to know why, and get it changed. Next, I would burn the hell out of foods in the toaster oven. I would leave the food in there purposefully and go away so they would burn. I would season everything black with pepper. I'd get loads and loads of black coffee, very hot, to kill my taste buds. Nurses would look in and say, "How are you doing?" I would pretend that I was eating and hide my peppered food from them. When they left, I would throw some more down the toilet. I'm surprised that I did not plug it.

They would come back, and my tray would be empty. I knew they would wonder about that, but they didn't say anything. I would get ravishingly hungry at night, and I knew where the kitchen was, so I would sneak down at night and get cookies or cornflakes or vegetables, or whatever, take some, and then sneak back upstairs. I would also see my menu on the wall and cross out some things so the cooks would think the nurses did it. Mom tried so hard to get me everything I wanted, and I wasted it all. I told her that too, but I think she knew before I told her. I stayed up as late as I wanted and got up as early as I wanted. I had as many visitors as I wanted and went out on passes just about as much as I wanted. Many people came to visit me and brought me stuff and food. I would throw the food away and feel guilty about what they had brought whenever I looked at it.

When I was in there, all of my teachers came to see me. I missed a lot of schoolwork because they didn't want to send it to me. The principal from school who used to teach psychology and studied psychiatry in university told my classmates what was wrong with me and why I was in there. They were all shocked, and many classmates, including a former best friend and a past boyfriend, felt guilty, like this disease was their fault. I felt bad about that.

When my family would come and we would plan to go out for supper or out on a pass, I would starve myself (no food or liquids) all day because I would rationalize that "I'll be hungry when we go out." Sometimes I would almost pass out, and I fell down the hospital stairs once. My legs were so weak, I couldn't even carry a bag up the stairs.

I had a boyfriend. Mom and Dad told him I was in the hospital because I had anorexia. He treated me as he saw me, and according to how I acted: like a baby. He babied me to no end and let me do, have, or say anything I liked. I liked that for about the first four weeks while I was in the hospital. I had dated him for about five weeks before I was admitted to the hospital. After a while I lost interest in him, and believe it or not, I asked him if he wanted to break up. He said that he did. I don't blame him. My mood swings were hard to judge. I have only seen him once since then, and he has another girlfriend. He was a very shy and caring guy, and I feel guilty because I wasted his time.

When I went back to school, at first, I was supposed to eat my lunch at the hospital. Mom must have thought I had eaten everything at the hospital, because she sent me sandwiches, cookies, fruit, etc. I would eat very little of it because no one was watching me eat. I would shove it in my school bag or lunch bag even though I was surrounded by doctors and nurses. I walked up to the hospital from school, going blocks and blocks out of my way. Many people that Mom and Dad know saw me. They would report back to Mom and she would give me heck at home. Not really "heck," but she would say, "I know you did that, but why?" Sometimes she would cry. We would sometimes just hold each other and cry.

Guilt

Dad would usually just be silent, but he knew. This made me feel guilty. My sister Catherine was so worried that she could hardly continue at university and did not want to come home. Relatives stayed away because they didn't know what to say or do, or they were just frustrated. Mom and I sometimes sat on her bed and just held hands and cried. We prayed a lot too. We have never been a really religious family, but those days we prayed out loud to ask God for help. We went to church a lot more, but God was a threat to me because I knew He could help me, but I didn't want help yet. My sister gave me this poster with "Footprints in the Sand" on it. It is a beautiful story about a man who wonders why during the worst parts of his life there was only one set of footprints when God was supposed to be with him during all of his life. God says that "During the worst points in your life, it was then that I carried you." I love that poster. I think I will make one like it myself tonight and put it up on this pin board.

Keep me from deceitful ways; be gracious
to me and teach me your law.

Psalm 119:29

Journaling: letters home

Dear Mom and Dad,
   I was thinking a lot today and felt like writing you. I was thinking about how cute and young you looked, Mom, when you put on the clothes you got for Christmas and how much your eyes sparkled. I remember you, Dad, when you put on your new shirts, and how good you looked. I remember when you bought those sweet Santa cups, and I broke them in my

haste to put them away; they made me worried! I know how embarrassed you both were when you made palacsinta at the table there and I wouldn't even have one. I knew how you felt then too, but it (anorexia) was out of control. Thank you to both of you for helping me through Christmas.

I must admit that I put a lot of love into those gifts I made for you both. You probably already know that. I really did.

You know, when I was packing to come here, I really did want yours and Catherine's help, Mom. I really did, but I just was not able to reach out and ask you. I didn't want to be alone then. I couldn't even meet your eyes, Mom, as I was walking out the door, because if I would have, I probably would have started crying and decided not to go. I miss your hugs most of all. We could hug all day, couldn't we? We will when I get home.

Dad, the hug you gave me when you left me here meant so much to me. And how you called me "dear" and asked me if I would be okay. My first few days here were the worst. Remembering what we talked about on the way here in the car, and when you left — that's what kept me going.

I'm sorry my letter today is so sad. It hasn't been such a good day. It's bad when you get your hopes all built up high, and things don't turn out like you expect. I'll be in here longer than I thought. Maybe until March sometime. I'll be on bedrest for two more weeks. I thought I would be off of it on Sunday. That means three meals and eight snacks a day for that long, too. I thought it would gradually lessen already. I thought I only had to be 105 pounds. Now it looks like it has to be 110 or 115 pounds. I don't know if I'm ready for that yet. Do you know what it's like to eat, and have to eat, and eat, and eat, and never be really hungry? I do. But I still carry on because it's working. Dr. Thomas is a very brilliant man. I really believe what he says.

Guilt

You know, I pray a lot. Because I do, I know that being here is the right thing to do. I know it for sure. I know that you both are probably praying for me too. I don't know if they would let me have letters from you yet. Maybe just let it be one-way communication for a while. At least I can talk to you openly this way. I love you both so much. I got a letter from Marcy. It was nice. It seemed like she didn't know what to say. I don't think I'll write her back yet. I'll write more later. Maybe tomorrow will be a better day!

Search me God, and know my heart; test
me and know my anxious thoughts.

Psalm 139:23 (NIV)

Dear Mom and Dad,

Hi! Thanks for phoning Dr. Thomas on Friday. I'm glad you did. Now I don't have to worry so much about school. I miss you both so much! I miss the farm, the house, my room, the dogs, Rusty, and even school a bit. I've been reading a lot lately — good thing I brought some good books. I think I'll have to get my eyes checked, because I think I need a stronger right contact lens. Was that the one that was just changed? I also need some contact stuff, and maybe a bit of money for things. Could you send some to Catherine for me? It makes me so happy when she phones or visits; it's some contact with my family.

Patients here sometimes come in and visit for a while, and I talk a bit with my nurses. I have some pretty good friends here. They are older than me. One girl who is 19, one married lady who is about 23 with a kid, and another lady who is 30 (and looks 15) with a kid. They're all bulimic. Another new girl who came in today is bulimic also. I don't know her yet. A girl who has migraine headaches — her name is Gwen — is super nice too. I also have a good friend here — his name's Gerald — he's 23, and good-looking! He sneaks in to visit me sometimes and we talk, and tonight he snuck in a chocolate Hershey's kiss for me! He's really sweet. Imagine me getting tied up with a guy in the psych ward...as if I don't have enough problems...excellent.

My roommate here is a bit strange. I wrote about her on another paper. I'll give it to Catherine to send to you. Writing to you guys is just like talking, but no one answers. I can imagine what you'd say though. I have to be on bedrest for about another week — longer than I thought. But I'll be okay. I also have to stay in longer than I thought. Dr. K told me that a good estimate is March. Don't worry, I promise you that I won't get "fed up" and leave. I have to weigh 110. I'm getting used to the idea now. It's no big horrendous issue like it was before. I hope you kept some tags from my jeans in case they don't fit me anymore so you can return them. Dr. K said that my body will even out over time. I really love you guys and I miss you. I'm doing okay though. I really have something here giving me strength. Catherine's minister came here to see me once. He's a really nice guy. He said he will come and visit me again.

I really feel like writing, so I'll outline my typical day here, so you can picture me now while you are reading this letter.

7:00 a.m. - Get woke up, go to bathroom, BP, weight, pulse checks. Wash, dress, fix bed, wait.

8:10 - Breakfast (good food here!) (for breakfast, anyway) Eat, lie on bed, doze.

9:30-10:00 - Dr. Thomas comes, we talk, and he does hypnotism sometimes. (Get this, he's doing breast enlargement on me!)

10:00 - Snack! Lie on bed, doze.

11:00 - Snack! Lie on stomach on bed, doze or sleep.

12:00 - Lunch (quite good lunches, new things I've never tried before like sardine and deviled eggs salad plate). Sleep, lying still on back.

2:00 - Snack! (I get to choose them all) Doze or read or draw or color.

3:00 - Snack! (as above)

4:00 - Snack! (as above) Lie on stomach, doze or sleep.

5:10 - Supper. (They aren't that great. Example: Shepherd's pie - yuck!) Lie on back, do self-hypnosis (I'm getting good!) or sleep.

7:00 - Snack! Read and rest.

7:30 - Fill out menu for next day.

8:00 - Snack! Read and rest.

9:30 - Snack. Read and rest and write.

10:00-11:00 - Go to bed.

So that's my day. Pretty exciting. It will be better when I'm out of this stupid bed, though. I finally could get my hair washed after 23 days, and I may get a tub-bath Monday instead of a bed-bath, so things are looking up. I'm through the worst part, anyways. Well, that's all I better write for now. Please take some pictures on my camera of you guys when you get all dressed up for something or when you do something that you think I'd like to see. Take some of the dogs too, and Rusty, please. I don't know if you should write yet, maybe wait another week. I can hardly wait to go home. I miss you both so much. I wish I could send you hugs, and you could send me some. I miss them. I love you. Bye-bye for now. Love and kisses. P.S. Could you please send me some shampoo and cream rinse? PSS My new nickname: "Bedsore."

"You have been a refuge for the poor,
a refuge for the needy in their distress,
a shelter from the storm
and a shade from the heat..."

Isaiah 25:4 (NIV)

Surrender

Surrendering Anorexia

At my lowest time, I finally surrendered the disease, my body, my mind, my past, present, and future to God. I knew He would heal me. I had known it all along. The doctors and nurses were His vessels, His ships carrying supplies and completing His wishes.

Every day I journaled prayers, asking God to get me through the challenge of the moment, and thanking Him for saving me. I eventually was able to see outside of myself and pray for those around me:

> *Please help me, Lord, to make it through this dinner hour okay. I'm calling on you for strength and willpower to help me, Lord, now. Please help me, because I need your strength, Lord.*

> *Lord, please help me. The afternoons are very long, and I try to find things to do. I hope I can color. Lord, thank you for keeping me calm. I can get better; it's not that hard. All I need is a strong mind and lots of willpower and determination. Thank you, Lord, for your many blessings. I know now that I am worthy of them.*

> *Everything will be okay now; I just know it. Thank you, Lord, for blessing me so richly. Thank you for guts and brains and willpower.*

Please help me do and say the truth, the right things, when I talk to the doctor and nurse. Give me strength, wisdom, and knowledge, Lord. Thank you, Lord. Give me calmness and strength. Please, Lord.

Thank you, Lord. Now everything will be okay. I have the Lord sitting here with me, and he'll be in the dining room with me too. Thank you, Lord, for being with me now and always to guide me and keep me.

Lord, I know you are here beside me. Thank you for giving me strength when I was talking to the doctor and nurse. Please bless that bulimic girl. Please give me strength and determination to get through this. I pray for strength from you. This is the right thing to do. I know that it is the right thing to do. Please forgive my sins and continue with your blessings. Help me to get some knowledge of your life by reading the Bible. I hope it will enlighten me. I would like to read the Christmas story first, and then I'd like to read some place that talks about "in difficult times." There will be comfort there, I know it. Thank you, Lord, for your many blessings. I know that I am worthy of them.

Help me to understand Your words when I read them in the Bible. Help me to believe Your words and trust in You. The sooner I get well, the sooner I can get on with my life. It's about time. Too many wasted days. Two wasted years fighting and arguing with myself. And I'm the worst person to argue with because I am so stubborn! I won't let this get me down. Just like when I would not stop when I was walking and running and go home. Or I wouldn't stop skipping. I just wouldn't. I won't stop now either.

Isn't that sad when I think back to all those times, hiding food, throwing it away. I'd not even look at anything — just get rid of it. Isn't that sick? The terrible mind battles. They were terrible. I will never forget them. I will never let them happen again. I don't need that.

Give me the strength to make it through each day here. Give me strength to take one day at a time and live for each day. Give me willpower and strength and stubbornness and determination, because that is what I have to call on now to survive here. Please give me creativity to keep drawing. Help me to adapt to myself and this way of life. I've come this far; I don't want to go back. I cannot go back. The Lord helps those who help themselves. Help me and give me strength and determination to make it through each day here. Thank you for helping me get this far and please help me continue on my road to success. I know that you are sitting here beside me and are there beside me in the dining room too when I need you. I need you. Thank you for helping me to call on you and trust in you. Lord, please give me strength. Please help me to help myself. Now is my chance. Thank you, Lord.

Please help me to show the doctor and nurses that I don't lie anymore. Help me to prove it to them and be strong and have guts. I know that I am worthy of your blessings.

Lord, please, this is a small setback. Please help me to do what's right. Give me calmness and wisdom to deal with this. Please help me get over this rut that is in the way, Lord. Please advise me and show me the way through this. I need your help and strength, Lord. Please show me the way and I will follow you. The Lord helps those who help themselves. I will help myself, Lord. I will. Give me strength.

Bless that beautiful man who prayed for me today. Thank you, Lord. Thank you so much. He is a beautiful person. He said, "God knows what she is thinking." God does know. You do know, Lord. Thank you, Lord.

Lord, please help me make it through the night tonight. Thank you for helping me to get better, Lord. This is the biggest thing I have ever done for myself, Lord. Thank you for your strength that you give to me, Lord. Thank you.

Thank you, Lord, also for the nosebleed. Thank you. I know it is a good sign. Thank you.

Thank you for helping me adapt to my changing body and accept myself. Please help me to keep my faith in You strong, and to remember to pray for your guidance. Please help me to figure out what's right and wrong with hypnosis. Lord, help me to do what's right according to you. Please keep me worthy of your blessings and help me to remember to pray to you in times of trouble.

Please help me to keep my faith strong in you and remember Dr. Thomas's words: stay on bedrest, eat 18 meals, no visitors. Accept these and you will beat anorexia.

Please help others in need like that poor girl and that poor bored guy who is wandering around here.

Thank you for my weigh-in this morning. Help me not to be scared of it. It is a mere, mere amount. Thank you, Lord, for your continued progress. Please give me strength and determination to make it through today. Give me willpower and help me to remember what Dr. Thomas said about the changes in my body and help me to think about them a lot.

Thank you for helping me make the doctor laugh.

Thank you for each new day and for continued progress of this chart. Please help me keep my faith in you strong, Lord, and never give in to this disease. Help me to know what I'm eating and want what I am eating. It doesn't hurt to smile any more. Lord, thank you!

Thank you for helping me recall what it was like back home.

Thank you, Lord, for helping me to feel better. For the cold cloth on my forehead and going to the bathroom. I believe and trust in you, Lord. And I know that everything will be okay, Lord. I just know it. Please help me to help this headache go away. I know it will. It's a sign from my body that things are going better.

Thank you, Lord, for your help and for giving me strength to get through all of this. Please forgive my sins, Lord. Let me do your will and what is right, God. Thank you, Lord. Please give me strength, Lord.

Thank you, Lord, for all of your many blessings. I thank you for getting me through this day. Thank you for your strength and guidance when I was talking to the doctor. Lord, please help me to get well. Lord, please take this headache away soon. I know that it is here for a reason, and I will see that reason soon.

I often wrote, "The Lord helps those who help themselves." I had no idea at the time that "God helps those who help themselves" is not actually a quote from the Bible. In fact, the Bible is more supportive of God helping those who are helpless, weak, and lost, especially in the context of salvation. God reached down and picked me up when I was hitting bottom. Just in time. To me, this prayer meant that even though I had been saved, I still needed to do my part to recover. God had given me a second chance to live, and I had to accept it, hold on tight, and fulfill the purpose He has for me.

Rejoice always, pray continually, give thanks in all circumstances; for this is God's will for you in Christ Jesus.

1 Thessalonians 5:16-18 (NIV)

Psychodrama

Several treatment modalities were used when I was in City Hospital, the most interesting being psychodrama. This is what I wrote about it.

> Psychodrama is an experience unlike any I have ever experienced. At this time, I am puzzled and don't know what to make of it. I will try to define and describe psychodrama and talk about some of the people that attend it.
>
> Psychodrama is scheduled for every Wednesday night and Saturday morning for about two hours. It is a group meeting that takes place on the fourth floor of the hospital. I have only attended two meetings since I was admitted. The sessions are conducted by Dr. K. Thomas.
>
> Before the meeting begins, people file into the large, open room and sit on the chairs backed up against the wall. There is a lot of tension in the air. People of all kinds and ages file in, but we all have something in common: an eating disorder. In psychodrama, we discuss our eating disorders and delve into the depths of our subconscious to try to discover what causes this disorder and how it affects our lives. The impact of our illness is revealed to us, and we are given solutions and hope to overcome our sicknesses. This is all done mainly through hypnosis. Dr. K leads us into a complete state of relaxation in which, in the first session, we were taken back to our birth. We were told to remember events in our lives step-by-step backwards, like a clock running the wrong way. We were told that

we were meant to be born. We were made to feel worthy of being alive. We all relived events in our lives at each age, up to the present time. This was done to learn if any secrets should come out that may have triggered our eating disorders. While this is happening, we are all in a very relaxed state. Everyone has their eyes closed and we are sitting back in our chairs or many prefer to lie flat on the floor as if asleep.

The whole point of hypnosis is to convince us that we are worthy to be born and that we have control over our own bodies. Eating disorders occur mainly because we believe that we cannot control our bodies. The longer a person has the disorder, the more that fear grows. It leads to health problems that can be very serious, and permanent psychotic problems, if you let it control you.

In my second session of psychodrama, we all lied on the floor at first. Dr. K told us to focus our attention on the girl sitting next to him. She looked to be about 20 years old, and was friendly, slightly overweight, and looked very tired. Dr. K proceeded to tell us that this girl (Judy) was completely under his control. He said that anything he tells her to do, she will do, as long as she agrees to it. He said that his tone of voice alone hypnotizes her. Judy began to yawn and asked him to hurry and give her permission to be hypnotized. He did, and after a few minutes her eyes closed, and her head dropped to her chest. One girl lifted her arm, and it was limp and heavy. She looked completely relaxed. Dr. K explained that because we have control over our own bodies, if he told us that we would not feel pain, we wouldn't. To demonstrate, Dr. K told the girl to make her hand feel apart from her body at the wrist. The hand was no longer to be a part of her. She agreed. He took out a sterile alcohol prep pad and rubbed a spot on her hand between her forefinger and her thumb. All the while, he was gently rubbing her hand. He took a needle out of his other pocket, uncapped it, and stuck it into her hand. He left it there, pointing out of her skin. There was very little blood. Dr. K took the needle out and put a bandage on her hand. He asked Judy to wake up at the count of three, if she agreed. At three, she woke and stretched, rubbing her eyes. She looked at the bandage on her hand, puzzled, and asked Dr. K what he had done to her. He explained and although she looked surprised, she was not upset. Apparently, he has done things like this to her many times in the past. Then he discussed the power of the mind and how a lady once cured herself of epilepsy and bulimia, and another lady cured her own mouth cancer. He showed us pictures of these people. He also showed pictures that he took of me when I was first admitted to the hospital. My nose was purple, and my hands were misshapen and discolored.

The final part of the session was to tell us not to try and figure out our illness. He demonstrated why using two group attendees. He placed chairs back-to-back in the middle of the floor and asked two people with bulimia to sit in them. One person was to be the side who was sick with bulimia who does not want help. That is the bad side. The other person was the good side, fighting to get better. The two people spoke their thoughts out loud, bickering back and forth, with Dr. K occasionally adding in ideas and points. The rest of us were asked to close our eyes and concentrate. It was interesting to hear and an obvious outlet for both participants. After this, the session was over and I was left with a sense of confusion, wondering if this was really happening.

Seventy-five percent of the people who attended the meetings have faces as white as this sheet of paper. Many wear makeup that looks colored on with crayons. Half of the people have thin, unhealthy-looking hair. Dr. K has told me about a girl who is also inpatient. Her name is Rachel, and she is about 20 years old. She used to climb the Rocky Mountains. She has bulimia and was taking illegal drugs. Her hair is a pale brownish-yellow color, her face is pale and blotchy, and she is average weight and size. She looks weak and walks bent over. She does not smile much and looks like there is something wrong with her jaw. She has had severe bulimia and been in the hospital for a long time. When she was brought in, she needed four nurses to hold her down because her whole body was cramping so badly. Her eyes were rolled upwards, and her mouth was open, with her tongue hanging out, head back, and neck stiff. Her back was arched with her arms and legs sticking up straight and toes pointed and overlapping each other. An electric shock machine was brought in to bring her out of it. After that she was sore, and her body ached so much that she stayed curled up in the fetal position in the corner almost all the time. She was up now, and even able to go out on pass. She played the good side of the bulimia skit in psychodrama.

Another girl walked into the session with a cane, and it looked like she has a clubfoot. She is medium build and her skin is pale. She told us that she has epilepsy. She works construction, recently got hit by a car, and she has bulimia. And we think we have problems?

Another girl is Mia, and she looks about my age. Her skin is snow-white, and she has thin orange-red hair. She is very thin. I later learned that she is 30 years old and the mother of a five-year-old. It's obvious that she doesn't want to get better. "Everyone is always telling me to gain weight," she whines. She is not married. She sits on the floor with her legs crossed or bent up to her chest. At first, she had anorexia, but now also has some combination of bulimia-anorexia.

Another girl whose name is Michelle is in her 20s but looks about 16 years old. She has had bulimia for a few years and is very bizarre. She is a belly dancer. She sits or lies on the floor and often cracks her neck, arms, shoulders, and legs.

She is very outspoken and has been a patient of Dr. K for a long time. She talks openly about her illness, and she and Dr. K shared this story. On the way to an appointment with Dr. K, she binged. She told Dr. K this when she arrived. He asked her if she wanted to vomit, and she said yes. He asked if she wanted him to go with her and she said yes. He went with her to the bathroom and asked her questions as she was vomiting, and he tape recorded the session. He said he would play that tape for us at some point. I'm not anxious to hear it. She was not ashamed at all to tell us that she does peculiar things while she vomits, such as scratching her head until it bleeds. I noticed that during psychodrama she is picking scabs off of her head.

Another woman at psychodrama claims to have delusions. She dresses in tight pants and high heels and carries a big purple handbag. Her hair is short and jet black and makeup is plastered on her white face. Dr. K asked her to tell us a little about her illness. She told us this: "I just have trouble swallowing so I only eat breakfast, coffee, and I drink juice the rest of the day." She doesn't think that is a problem and sat quietly all through psychodrama.

Another lady who is also inpatient has had bulimia for four years, and she has a jaw problem and a lisp, probably as a result of vomiting. She told me she is always exhausted. She is married with two children.

Ann is in her 40s and is the oldest person in group. She had anorexia and now has bulimia. Her skin is very while and she has dark, hollow eyes. She told us that she was recently in a car accident and needed to have plastic surgery on her face, so it is badly scarred.

Another girl admitted yesterday has had bulimia for three years. She is a first-year medical student. She seems motivated to overcome the disorder, and I hope she makes it.

Psychodrama

Everyone at psychodrama has bulimia, had anorexia in the past, or has a combination of both. They are very sick people. Dr. K told me that most of them vomit 15 to 20 times a day. They all trust Dr. K completely. Many of the girls are very pretty and they seem to know it on the outside, but I guess that inside they do not. Most have tried to commit suicide.

Psychodrama is a very controversial and puzzling thing to me. Maybe after more sessions I will gain a better understanding of it.

Do not conform to the pattern of this world, but be transformed by the renewing of your mind. Then you will be able to test and approve what God's will is — his good, pleasing and perfect will.

Romans 12:2 (NIV)

People on the Psych Ward

The weeks spent in the hospital were both scary and interesting. When I wasn't focused on my own healing, I began seeing the circumstances and struggles of other people, and I felt a little more normal. Here are some of their stories.

The other day a boy came in my room. He is about 6 feet 2 inches. He has shoulder-length dark hair and dark eyes. He was very quiet when the nurses were showing him around. He looks about 18 or 20 years old. He wears normal clothes, jeans and a t-shirt. He walks by my room to get to his room. He walked by many times when he first came in. He always looked in, but never smiled. I try to smile or wave at everybody who walks by. The third time he stared in, I did not smile but looked back at him, puzzled. The fourth time he walked right into my room and stood just inside the door.

"Debbie?" he said. "Debbie??" he asked louder. He wasn't smiling, and his eyes were large and dark. I almost peed the bed. "I'm not Debbie," I squeaked out. He looked shocked. "Oh, I'm sorry," he said quickly and walked out. He still looks into my room now and then but never smiles. I don't smile at him either. Today he got a personal sitter. He must either be suicidal or a violent maniac, that's what I think... crazy!

There's another boy in here. He sneaks in and talks to me quite a bit. He told me his name, but I forgot. He said he is 24 years old. He is about 6 feet tall, with nice, shoulder-length, sandy hair. He has a kind face and sad eyes. He is interested in art and showed me a drawing that he did. It's very neat. It was done on large pastel paper. It is copies of the same picture, framed, one behind the other, in different sizes. I like it a lot. I showed him some of my work. He waves and says something nearly every time he walks by.

    Now I have a roommate. Her name is Annie. I've traded places with Sharon. Sharon can't even walk to the bathroom by herself. Dr. Thomas told her that she will die. It is very disturbing to hear. Annie is 81 years old. She is about 4 feet 10 inches tall with salt-and-pepper streaked shoulder-length straight hair. She is small and stooped over and walks dragging her feet slowly. She always wears a plaid men's black and gray work shirt buttoned up over an old white blouse and black stretch pants with one side hemmed. She is from a small town where her husband is in the nursing home. She lived alone in her own house. She has never locked the doors. She hardly uses any electric heat because she is scared that it will burn down the house. She has a small wood-burning stove. She was not taking care of herself; she ate bread but that's about it. She is very skinny. She never washed, bathed, or anything. She grew a large moustache and beard. When she came in, she hadn't bathed or changed her clothes for months. She has big balls on her work socks that have been darned over and over. Her dresses are cut up, sewn together blue jeans. She has two of them. That's all. Her panties are cut-off blue jeans. Her bras were ancient relics.

    The story is that she was told by the public health nurse that she would be brought here on Christmas Eve and not allowed to live alone there anymore. It was for her own good. She put up a big fight with the cops and fought them all the way here. Now she only has a moustache and two sets of clothes that she has to change into every second day. She feels very sorry *for herself and told me that she will never forgive the public health nurse.*

Laura came in two weeks before I did. She is very pretty. She is 22 years old. She came in because her boyfriend broke up with her. She says he used her. She was very upset, but I don't think she was suicidal. She made me a penholder. She was a good friend. She was released on January 9th. She was very happy when she was released. In here, she was quite moody at times but good to talk to at other times.

Keo is a pregnant Chinese girl who is 22 years old. She came in about two days after I did. She is short with a tummy. She doesn't speak, read, or write English very well. She is very friendly and comes in my room to visit me whenever she walks by. She is dying to get out. Her husband signed her in because she throws awful, violent screaming temper tantrums at him. He works here at the hospital on a different floor as a janitor. We always discuss the menus and talk about what's good and what isn't. She brought me homemade Chinese food once, but the nurses would not let me eat it because they don't know exactly what's in it. She is about 5 feet tall and is really cute. She has two cute little kids. The kids and her husband visit her every night and when they don't, she goes out on a pass.

Harry is a man who is about 72 years old. He has Alzheimer's disease. He has the room next to me on the right. He is very mixed-up, but such a cute old man. He needs to be tied to his chair sometimes, and when he is, he shakes it and shakes it. His family visits about every third day. Once he said very loudly, "There's no room in the basement!" just out of the blue. Then he said, "Hey! There's no room in the basement!" He heard no reply except for giggling at the nurse's station. One nurse said, "Well, don't worry, because there's lots of room upstairs!" Another said, "Or you could always sleep on the couch in the living room!" It was hilarious, and I could not stop laugh-

ing. Harry always has gas. Once he came into my room with a Safeway shopping bag and asked me, "What do you have to put in here?" I gave him a napkin. Then he closed the bag and left. Another time he came in, straightened my blankets, and sat down at the foot of my bed. He watched me color until he got bored and left. He's always trying to open and close doors. He borrowed my pencil once to pick the lock on the fire doors. He came into my room tonight and was searching behind my door. "Harry, what are you looking for?" I asked. "Pen nibs, and nibs and racing cars!" He replied with a grin.

Joe is an old man about 70 years old. He always comes right into my room, pulls up a chair and sits down. He walks slow and bent over, except for one day when he said, "Maybe I'll walk fast today. Yeah! That's what I'll do! Maybe then I won't be so depressed!" So, he did for one day. He marched straight and lifted his knees high, up and down the hallway. He seemed to be in a good mood. Yesterday he asked me, "Have you ever had an ECG?" "Yes", I said, "about a year ago." "Well, does it last long?" he asked. "Yeah, it lasted this long." I said, meaning that I have not needed another one since, not meaning to confuse him… but I did. "Where did they put it?" he asked. I replied, "Put what?" "Where did they put it, on your pacemaker? I have to get one, and I want to know if they attach it to my pacemaker." I told him I didn't know because I don't have a pacemaker. "How big is it? I'm worried about it," he said. "Oh, don't worry. It's nothing, "I said. "It's only about this big." I made a small circle with my hand. "Where does it go?" he asked. "Oh, right about here," I pointed to my chest. "How deep do they cut?" he asked me. "Oh, it's just like when you cut your finger," I replied, "not deep at all." "Are you okay since?" "Dandy!" I replied. "Never been healthier!" "Will it get rid of my depression?" he asked. "Oh, for sure!" I said. This seemed to satisfy him, and he left.

I don't know her real name, but I'll call her Cloris. She told me that she gets a lot of headaches. She has dark circles under her eyes and is about 25 years old. Cloris found out two days ago that she has a blood clot at the back of her brain. Now she always has a headache.

Debbie arrived two weeks before Christmas. She was supposed to be let out two days ago, but she refused to go. She said she is "not ready." She is afraid to be alone. She has never gone shopping or to a show alone, or even had a room by herself. She loves it here. She is protected and warm, with three meals and others around her all the time. She is on the phone talking and laughing with friends most of the time. She reads love novels spread out on her couch in the TV room and runs back and forth to her room doing imaginary tasks. She dramatizes everything. A big day for her is when she goes for a walk in the afternoon. She wears trendy, preppy clothes and struts around in a sweater, skirt, and high heels on Sundays. She doesn't go to church and seems to have no desire to. I can't figure her out. I'll probably be out of here before she is!

Sister Mary is a nun. She is about 80 years old. She has cropped white hair. She is very short and slim when you look at her from the front, but from the side she looks about ready to have a baby! She is so cute. Tonight, she came into my room and gave me a peppermint. When she walks, it is different. She shuffles along quickly, dragging her feet. Her legs move, her arms and hands wave along every which way, her neck moves back and forth, her head moves, her eyes open and close, her mouth moves, and she slurps and grunts! She looks and walks a lot like E.T (from the movie). I heard that she is in here because she beat up some nuns at the convent!

Suzanne is on her tenth admission. She has anorexia. She looks like I do in jeans, only maybe not quite as bad. I think the nurse said she is 30 years old, but she looks and acts like a child. She is like a living image of me last year when I was in the hospital. The nurses here allow her to pass out menus daily and do all little odd jobs. She is treated special, and always hangs around at the nurse's station, talking, joking, laughing loudly, and trying to fit in. She tells jokes to draw attention to herself. She usually wears a lot of dark blue eyeshadow and resembles my last year high school picture.

She went to church this morning. She was the only one on the ward that went. Suzanne walks up and down the hallways here. Up and down, back and forth, so many times. I noticed that before I was put on complete bedrest. She walked by my door much more often than she does now. I watch her walk by and she sees me watching and gives a very broad, fake smile. She walks back and forth, and up and down. There is no place she is going, and I noticed that she walks a lot more after mealtimes. I wonder why.

I feel sorry for her and wish I could help, but I'm afraid it's already too late for her. Obviously, no one can help her. But I still wish I could offer her some strength, you know? Here is a bit of history that Dr. Thomas and the head nurse told me. She has been admitted here 10 times, but this time is probably her last. She is getting released soon. When she came in, she weighed 70 pounds. They had to lift her from bed to chair. She had collapsed somewhere and that's why she was brought in. She was walking 25 miles a day around the perimeter of the city. She has no hips, thighs, or bust. I know what she does, because I was her. Yesterday morning I heard her talking to the nurses: "I know what I should do! I should go visit my friend. I haven't seen her in ages! Or should I go see my other friend and we will go for coffee somewhere? Oh no, maybe I should phone. Or she might be going away for the weekend." This monologue went on for a while until she was let out on a pass. She was gone from about 1:30 p.m. until 4:30 p.m.

Dinner is at 5 p.m. When she came back, she was high on exercise. If anyone can tell that, I can. She was bubbling over with excitement, standing at the desk, talking to the poor nurses. She was telling them ecstatically about how pretty and nice her friend is, and that her friend had even put on weight. The nurses nodded and commented, trying to act engaged.

Suzanne doesn't eat with anyone. She eats alone in her room. I wondered if she had actually gone to see her friend, or if she just went for a walk, run, jog, etc., the whole time. She speaks dramatically and falsely, probably a lot like I did. I can almost feel the fatigue in her legs after her long walks. When she came back from the pass yesterday, she was walking slower than usual and wearing slippers over socks. She usually wears running shoes (because she probably thinks, as I did, that you can walk faster and use up more calories wearing them). I would be interested to see the bottoms of her feet as there are probably callouses on them. She took a long bath and then assisted the nurses and cleaning ladies to scrub down the bathroom afterwards. All too familiar. When given the choice, she chose to overcome anorexia "her way" versus what Dr. K recommended. That's why she isn't any better.

No one has ever seen God; but if we love one another,
God lives in us and his love is made complete in us.

1 John 4:12 (NIV)

Jeremiah 29:11

The last few weeks in City Hospital were at the same time exciting and terrifying. I had more privileges and freedom within the confines of the psychiatric ward, as well as outside of it. My sister was able to visit me, and I went on passes. I went outside for long walks and could walk around freely. I met a man who was admitted for drug addiction treatment. He and I would sit together, alone in the TV room some evenings, talking about random things. I felt my body wake up at the thought of being alone with him, even there in the TV room. He made me laugh sometimes and that felt surprisingly good.

The days were structured and predictable, and I had more energy and was thinking more clearly as each day passed. I grew accustomed to the routine and it became comfortable. At times I dreaded leaving the safe confines of the nursing unit and entering the real world outside of it. The real world was not structured, routine, or predictable. It wasn't safe and comfortable. I knew I had to leave there a mature young adult, ready to take care of myself, but I was afraid. Even though I knew God had saved me, He had a plan and purpose for me, and He had my back, my faith wavered, and I felt alone and afraid. Being in the psychiatric unit, or any area of a hospital, for that matter, seems like being in prison. The day is foreseeable and there are few surprises. You know that the basic necessities are taken care of no matter what: food, clothing, and shelter. You can rest in the knowledge that you will be safer inside than outside those walls. There is less access to people and things that are harmful, including drugs, alcohol, bad habits, addictions, and ways to self-punish. I was there. I was afraid to leave and face the scary unknown. As the days passed, I wondered if I was ready to face the real world, or worse…myself.

I held on to Jeremiah 29:11: "For I know the plans I have for you," declares the Lord, "plans to prosper you and not to harm you, plans to give you hope and a future." I knew that God's plans for me had not been fulfilled yet. In fact, His plans had only just begun. A new urgency replaced the apathy I had felt for years. I developed a yearning to leave that place, and learn what God had in store for me. I had no doubt that He would lay a perfect path before me to follow, and life would be easy from here on out. I left there with confidence, but this was coupled with a naiveté that would cripple me in the future.

For I know the plans I have for you," declares the Lord, "plans to prosper you and not to harm you, plans to give you hope and a future.

Jeremiah 29:11 (NIV)

Dr. K. Thomas notes:

Diagnosis on admission: Anorexia nervosa

Final diagnosis: Anorexia

Date of discharge: February 27, 1987

Jeremiah 29:11

Condition at discharge: Improved

Summary of case (condensed history)

This 17-year-old student was admitted for treatment of anorexia. Her symptoms were severe weight loss, amenorrhea, manipulative habits, poor interpersonal relationships, cold hands, bradycardia, and a denial of her illness. It took some time before she started gaining some insight and she was put to total bedrest, diet counseling and increasingly more food intake, psychodrama sessions, and group psychotherapy. Gradually, Adrienne put on 30 pounds of weight. In the beginning she had body image disturbances, but they improved as well. She was gradually mobilized and was able to maintain her body weight. Her family was also interviewed and further follow-up had been arranged. She has not had her periods yet, but it is expected that in the next couple of months with self-hypnosis she will be able to produce her periods.

Dr. Thomas is not a Christian. He follows a different religion and worships a different god. He was very involved in my treatment and I grew to trust him and believe in his plan to cure me. When I was first admitted, I was in a single room with a single bed in one corner. Right in my line of vision from the bed was a cork board and a graph. The horizontal axis was time in days up to 30 days, and the vertical axis was weight in pounds.

For the first few days the line was flat. When I prayed to God for help accepting the intensive treatment program, the graph started to change. Each morning, the nurses would weigh me and draw a line on the graph paper through the box for that day. The line went from the lower left corner to the upper right corner at a 45-degree angle. Each day was the same; a perfect 45-degree angle line grew longer as each day passed until it covered the entire graph. Dr. K came in to see patients on a Sunday afternoon at some point during that time. He looked at the graph for a while, and then remarked, "I don't know the God you serve, but keep believing in Him, because I have never seen progress like this before." I smiled, knowing that God had me right where He wanted me.

Therefore God exalted him to the highest place and gave him the name that is above every name, that at the name of Jesus every knee should bow, in heaven and on earth and under the earth, and every tongue acknowledge that Jesus Christ is Lord, to the glory of God the Father.

Philippians 2: 9-11 (NIV)

The Cleansing

This essay was written soon after I was discharged from City Hospital and returned home and back to my senior year in high school:

> Dad gently set my suitcases down and we stood facing each other in the small, clean room. I felt the tears well up in my eyes, and for the first time in a long time, I grabbed him and clung to him tightly, and he embraced me. Silent tears rolled down my cheeks.
> "Are you going to be okay?" he asked. "Yeah, I'll be okay," I replied weakly, trying to stifle my sobs. I impatiently wiped the silly, childish tears off my face and tried to look strong for Dad.
> "Well, I'd better be going. Bye, dear," he said. He turned and left quickly, but not before I saw his eyes glassy with unshed tears.
> He had closed the door on his way out, and I was left alone with anorexia. My tears dried and I felt that familiar, anxious, hyperactive feeling. Carefully I began to unpack my bags and hang clothes up the small closet. My stomach growled as I worked, and I experienced an indescribable feeling of power, which is typical of my sickness. I have anorexia nervosa, which is defined as "a persistent compulsive drive for thinness." It is emaciating, and in most cases, life-threatening.
> Shortly after I finished unpacking, I sat down on the roll-up hospital bed. Looking out the window at the Big City

Agencies building across the street, I didn't even notice a nurse enter behind me, until she spoke, saying she would like to give me a tour around the ward, and asking me if I would go with her. I agreed, and she showed me around the various rooms: the kitchenette, dining room, TV room, bathrooms, nurses' station, and recreation room. I didn't really hear her talking or understand what she was doing, I just blindly followed her.

Next, she led me into a small examination room and took my vital signs. My blood pressure was barely readable, my pulse almost nonexistent at 35 beats per minute. My weight was 81 pounds. The smiling nurse asked me many questions and I answered them mechanically. I only remember the final one: "Do you know where you are?" Laughing at her, I said, "The hospital!" Smiling politely, she led me back to my room and I sat down on the bed. I felt dizzy, yet so strong.

I didn't know at the time what caused me to say anything, but I blurted out a request for a sandwich. The fear of that food felt so real, and it was pounding in my head, and I dreaded the answer. The nurse casually agreed to the request and told me to please wait a few minutes and she would order one. She asked what kind I would prefer: beef, turkey, egg-salad, salmon, or cheese. I was stumped and fighting internally with myself. Feelings of anxiety as strong as the hunger gnawed away at my insides, but something stronger in me answered her and said "turkey." She nodded and walked away.

I looked down at my hands. They were deep purple and clenched tightly together, as if in prayer, on my lap. Was that the answer? Would prayer get me through this? I began to pray for strength, silently, simply, and repeatedly.

After a short time, the nurse returned, carrying my sandwich. She asked if I would like to go and eat in the dining room and I agreed. Food in hand, I followed her down the long narrow hallway.

When I entered, I saw a coffee perk, asked if I was allowed some coffee, and helped myself. I sat down at a table by myself and began the usual process of dismantling my sandwich. A young girl walked in and sat with me. She watched as I picked at my food. I prayed for strength before eating each small piece. The strength came and I managed to finish it, but the awful feeling of guilt was as strong as the feeling of pride that I had for being able to finish that sandwich. I remembered back to the last time I had eaten a whole sandwich like that, and it had been a very long time. The girl finally introduced herself and explained why she was in the psychiatric ward and what I was to expect in this place.

I was not listening. All I had on my mind was myself. Should I really have come here? All of my doubts disappeared as I again saw my cold, bony hands clasped tightly together. I knew that I had done the right thing, and I again prayed to God for help through this. I felt exhausted but also had a feeling of peace that I had never felt before. It felt new and good, and I went to bed.

The following four days went by in a blur. I went through many physical examinations and I was seen by numerous nurses, specialists, and dietitians.

I had to stay by myself in my room, and every day my psychiatrist asked me if I wanted to go home yet. He was testing me, and I knew it. I would answer a definitive "no," looking him right in the eye when I said it. I knew that a person really has to want to get better before they can. I did my best to do everything the staff told me to do. They told me that I could write, if I wanted to. So I started writing.

Every experience that had brought me shame, sorrow, and anguish that I had kept bottled up for so long came flowing out on to the paper. I wrote until I was exhausted, sweating, and sobbing. Over 30 pages of my secrets streamed on to paper. I was in a sort of trance, oblivious of people coming in and out of my room. My dam had finally burst, and I felt a weight lifted off my shoulders that I didn't even know was there. I wrote until I felt I had borne all, and my mind was relaxed. Then I would give the papers to the nurses, as if I were confessing every sin.

I wondered how long I would need to stay in the hospital. No one had given me any clue. My weight was recorded every day and had not changed since I arrived four days earlier. On New Year's Eve day, I was faced with my precepts. When Dr. Thomas came in for his daily visit, instead of coming alone he brought the head nurse with him. They closed the door and sat down facing me. They were expressionless, and I was terrified. I clenched my hands together and silently prayed for strength. The doctor asked me if I was wondering how long I would have to stay there, and I nodded. Then he asked me how long I wanted to stay. I replied, "As short a time as possible." Then he explained, "Okay, but you have two choices: either you can be in here for six months and put on weight at your own rate, or one month, doing it our way." My body tensed, but I knew the right answer. I looked at them and said, "Your way."

He explained their way. Complete bed rest, flat on my back, with no walking except to the bathroom in the room. The head of my bed would be rolled up for meals only. I would be allowed no visitors except the doctors and nurse, no phone calls, no television, radio, or books, or any other form of entertainment. He explained that any other entertainment would take my mind off my own problem. I was to constantly be thinking about my problem. I was allowed to do more writing or drawing if I wanted. I had to wear my nightclothes at all times, as well as gloves and socks, and stay beneath the covers. I had to be on hourly snacks, nine a day, plus three large meals. I could choose what I wanted for meals from a regular restaurant-

type menu and snacks from a list that had almost every kind of snack on it. I could not bathe or wash my hair, or even brush it on my own. The nurses would give me a daily bed bath.

After they finished, they again asked me if I wanted to leave. I was stupefied as they described what it would be like for me, and I prayed fervently and silently to make the right decision. Then I looked them in their eyes as power came from Another Source and I said, "No. I'll do whatever it takes." They looked at me as if surprised but quickly covered up their expressions and continued describing my treatment that would begin the following day. I just sat and listened.

After they left, I cried. It was a relief. I knew I had made the right decision to change my life, and I thanked God for it. The next day was New Year's Day. I was allowed to phone home for the last time. I only talked for 10 minutes and then had to go back to bed.

The next few days were very difficult. Staying in bed all day was bad enough, but the worst part was the amount of food I had to consume. I had been living on practically nothing before going into the hospital. It had gone from one extreme to the other. Thanks to the nurses who gently urged me on without pushing, I managed to consume all of the meals and snacks they provided. Amazingly, my feelings of guilt began to slowly dissolve. I did a lot of praying during those days.

After a while, immediately following the large meals, I could feel my heart beating rapidly inside my thin chest and pulse points throughout my body. My fingers and toes tingled and throbbed. I was amazed. I hadn't felt anything in my body for a long time. They were good, and I felt as if I was coming alive. These feelings encouraged me to keep on eating my meals. I would finish a meal and lie back in bliss, very aware of the stimulation going on all over my body. I could relax for an hour before my next snack arrived.

The nurses watched me closely and posted a large weight and vital signs chart above my bed, which was updated every morning. My doctor looked happy with my progress as he inspected the chart every day. He didn't work on my mental state of mind yet, he explained, because my brain was so malnourished, I would not understand him anyway. He was probably right. He took pictures of my nude form to keep in his files, answered my many questions, and even made a special trip up to the hospital on Sunday to see me. He taught me about hypnotherapy, using hypnosis to help cure me. In one session he made me use the power of my mind to change my hands, which were purplish-blue from lack of circulation, to a normal healthy color. I could then remove the gloves that I had to wear. My doctor was an amazing man, and I soon learned to just respect him, not fear him.

He explained all of the things I would feel as my body went through changes and my nerves, cells, bones, and skin were being rehabilitated. I was told that I would feel bloated and tired all of the time. I would get horrible migraine headaches for about a week, which would lead to gushing nosebleeds. My sinuses were being stimulated and rejuvenated. I would lose all of the fine hair which had grown to cover and protect my entire body from the cold, as well as the hair on my head. After about three weeks, my sweat glands would be activated and I would perspire profusely, and then I would be allowed out from beneath the covers, but I would still have to remain in bed. All of my senses would become clear and distinct, and I would have a jumble of thoughts going through my head.

All of these things happened during the next three weeks in succession, just as my doctor told me they would. Something held me back from fighting them, and I relaxed and allowed them to happen. I felt like I had surrendered myself over to these changes. When I felt panic and anxiety, I would pray and write. I realized that this was the greatest gift I could give myself. It was a cleansing which I had never experienced before, and I'm sure I never will again.

I was in bed for 29 days. In that time, I gained 30 pounds. As I watched myself gain the weight, I could see it go to different areas of my body. I can't say I was happy about it, but I just accepted it. That was in stark contrast to how I would have felt only four weeks earlier.

Once I was allowed up and out of bed, I was put in a wheelchair for four days and then allowed to walk short distances around the ward. I was informed that there was a good chance my heart would give out because I was not used to carrying all of the extra weight. I felt a few scary chest pains but nothing else happened, thank God. I was reminded again that God had plans for me after all of this was over. I eventually graduated to walking outside, up to two hours a day. It was so good to smell the crisp air outside!

I managed well during my last four weeks in the hospital. It was a crucial time because I could have fallen back easily if I chose to. I was released on February 27, 62 days after being admitted. During that time, my life changed dramatically. Almost completely. Although sometimes I still have the same old urges that would lead me right back to the state I was in the day I entered the hospital.

I can hardly imagine returning to that pitiful way of life where I was barely surviving. Now I know that I am stronger, both physically and spiritually. I try to live for today, yet still look forward to tomorrow. My family and most people that I see seem different now than before. They are real people, not just rocks. I saw them as cold, hard, and uncaring before. I look at things in a different light now. The hospital experience has opened my eyes to a lot of new things. The best two things I have learned are that you have to love yourself before you can love anyone else, and that God only helps those who help themselves.

<u>My English teacher wrote:</u>

This short story meets all requirements for a good piece of literature. You set up and inciting force, build up to a climax, and include descriptive terms on the many conflicts. Not only that, but the emotional aspect is very strong, which makes the main character very real and prominent. Well done!

These encouraging words reinforced my desire to write.

Come and hear, all you who fear God; let
me tell you what he has done for me.

Psalm 66:16

Recovery and Relapse

I left the hospital a different person. I knew there was a reason why I had come back from the depths of anorexia. I knew God had a plan and purpose for me.

I bought a magnet that said, "The world is your oyster." The quote is roughly taken from Shakespeare and has several interpretations. The meaning I like best is that although each oyster may hold a pearl, most do not. It takes perseverance, patience, and often hard work to find and pry open enough oysters to find a pearl, but it's worth it if you do. Although at that point in my life I had never seen an oyster and knew nothing about them, I felt renewed, reborn, exhilarated, and ready to go out into the world, searching for pearls.

I continued to see Dr. Thomas once a week at first and then less frequently as the months passed. He encouraged me to mold people out of clay so that we could further explore my altered body image. I would spend hours at home meticulously shaping fat and skinny women out of clay, air drying, and painting them to take them to my next appointment. My doctor asked me to leave them there. I'm not sure what he did with them, but there they were, sitting on his desk like old friends waiting for me at every appointment. During one of my last appointments, Dr. Thomas said something to me that I have held on to and repeated to myself ever since. He told me that I was so stubborn and determined that if I channeled it in the right direction, I could be successful in anything I set out to do.

I returned to high school to complete my senior year with three months left. The missed time from being in the hospital and the few years when I was in school but just existing as a shell of myself was apparent in my grades. Although I felt like the fog had lifted in my mind, I knew it would be a miracle if I passed and graduated. Classmates, teachers, and townsfolk looked at me with curiosity. I was 25 to 30 pounds heavier, and as weight gain goes, it had settled centrally: on my face, torso, and stomach. No one knew what to say, so most people said nothing. I understood, but loneliness was a constant companion. I kept my head down and focused on schoolwork. The only person I felt close to was my English teacher. I had shared my struggles and story with her through the essays I had written, and I felt like she understood me and I could trust her. I religiously following the eating and exercise program provided to me when I left City Hospital. The program, doctors, nurses, and most importantly, God, had saved me, so I wasn't about to take any chances.

I felt a renewed sense of purpose, strength, and urgency to achieve the short and long-term goals I had set for myself. Although I had gained weight and looked generally "normal," the personality traits of anorexia were still there. I yearned to have control over my future and planning it made me feel secure. In three months, I would finish high school. My goal was to get the hell off the farm and out of that town and as far away as I could, as soon as possible. My bags were packed. I was surrounded by people and memories of anorexia and I needed to move forward and shut the door on that part of my life.

In a small town where everybody knows everybody, there are a lot of favors. My teachers did a lot of favors for me, and I managed to complete my senior year with a C average and graduate with my peers. I was short math and science credits but knew I could make those up elsewhere, anywhere away from that town. I moved to the city and prepared to start university in the fall in pursuit of a Fine Arts degree. In defiance of when I was a child and Dad told me that my coloring "wasn't very nice," I chose to major in art. I believe that God places different passions in all of us, and if we tap into that and pursue it, we have the natural ability to succeed. A passion for life without fear of failure is liberating, and I moved forward as fast as I could.

The art classes, sculpting, and drawing seemed to be calling me. I believed that God had my life planned out for me and all I had to do was enjoy the ride. What was missing? Although my faith in God was rock solid, it lacked depth and understanding. I still did not know Jesus. That came later.

University began. I lived in an off-campus residence with five other gals that I didn't know. It was a multi-ethnic group: three of us white, an Asian girl, and a Korean girl. I took a part-time job in a deli across the river, attended classes, and swam in the campus pool. I took ballroom dance classes with a friend of a friend that I had a huge crush on and kept as busy as I could. I found my old habits, carefully watching what I ate and extending my exercise sessions. By October I had lost 10 to 15 pounds. Some of the same old anorexia feelings came back, including pride and relief in knowing that I could still lose weight so easily. At the same time, I was afraid of anorexia. I knew it was only a few bad decisions away. If I allowed it to come back, all the gifts God had given me would be thrown away and I would fit right in with most statistics; one in three people with anorexia relapse within a year of treatment, and only 50 percent recover.

Mom sent me a letter a few months after I was discharged from City Hospital. I am not sure why I kept it because I felt so frustrated reading it. Mom was a patient in the small-town hospital when she wrote it. She wrote, "They are excellent to me in here. I'm in a private room and I'm getting spoiled rotten! Dad came in yesterday to visit. Lisa brought me a rose and two carnations, a basket of fruit from Wilson's, a rose in a rose bowl from the union, mints and two mags from Marsha. Honestly, it's better than a birthday!"

This sounded so similar to what I wrote when I was admitted to the small-town hospital. I was thrilled with the attention to the point of being giddy. I loved all the gifts because it was all about me. I was the center of attention and loved that people went out of their way to show me that. Yes, there is a genetic basis for eating disorders and many other personality traits. In fact, heritability estimates include a risk up to 75 percent higher in children of adults with disordered eating conditions.

In the same letter, Mom claimed that she "knew there was something wrong" since Thanksgiving and had been very concerned since. She wrote that there was something she needed to tell me then but didn't know if she should. She said in her mind there is such a strong bond between us that she thinks she knows what I am feeling. She said, "I feel that you could be completely well but that you are hiding behind 'anorexia' as a shield from the real world because you are afraid of failure. You are insecure inside, and by having an illness to kind of blame it on, you feel that you are being shielded. If you could only 'escape' just once, I mean really start eating properly, three meals a day — who cares how many calories are in them — and feel so good you would never go back into your shell. I promise you that the real world isn't such a terrible place."

The words and behavior of a parent are internalized in a child for their entire life. I had heard, "I'm just going to eat healthy!" and "I'm going to start eating properly!" for most of my life. In fact, to this day when I eat dessert or something I "should not be eating" I hear my mother's voice saying that in my head. Mom implied that anorexia is not really a "thing" but just an excuse for me because I am so insecure. While it's true that poor self-esteem is a factor in anorexia nervosa, it's not all anorexia is. Anorexia is a disease that can control a person's life even to the point of taking it. Especially hypersensitive to criticism from the person closest to me, I allowed her words to cut deep.

Along with the weight loss came an oddly familiar discomfort in the area of my coccyx bone, plus a fever and general unwell feeling. When I was on bed rest in the hospital, I often found the only comfortable position was lying flat on my back, especially after I had eaten and felt bloated and full. I would lie still, praying and feeling the food digest. Because I ate so often, I was in this position a lot, and developed a stage three to four decubitus ulcer (bedsore). The sore was so deep it had reached the subcutaneous tissue and was approaching the bone. Although the ulcer had healed at the skin surface before I left the hospital, unbeknownst to the doctor or nurses the wound beneath had remained. Now several months later it had tunneled and was infected. I saw a doctor and had outpatient surgery to open and debride it. The tunnel had to be flushed, cleaned, and packed with new gauze every day. I couldn't see the wound to take care of it myself so I went home for a week. My mom lovingly took care of me. This time she gently expressed her concerns about my weight loss and this complication, but after a few days sent me on my way back to college. She knew that holding me back would only result in defiance and increase the likelihood of relapse. I heard her words and understood what was happening.

Letter from my dad sent about the same time:

> *Hi. How are you? I am sorry I can't go and see you. I hear you are having problems again. I thought you had it licked. My dear, I told you many times that you are the only one who can lick this problem. We can help, but it's up to you. For if you don't try very hard, you'll blow everything going for you! Your schooling, your boyfriend, and your future. I'm sick and tired of this disease. So, for God's sake, give it your biggest effort you ever did. I know you can lick it if you try. Remember that western song about the devil and the fiddle player. Dad loves you.*

My dad didn't talk without a good reason to, and he wrote even less. However, he read a lot. Any spare time was spent reading newspapers. It was a big deal for my dad to write this letter, and it came directly from his heart, as if he were speaking to me face-to-face. His wisdom shows as he turned my focus away from the present predicament, and toward what I valued, my future. I can't remember my dad ever saying that he was sick and tired of anything, so for him to say that struck a nerve. He helped me realize that my disease was also affecting him, and that made me think. Although he wasn't educated in psychology, he knew that anorexia is a battle of the mind and likened it to the song "The Devil Went Down to Georgia" about playing fiddle against the devil with the risk of losing your soul and winning the fight. My dad said he knew I could win the battle, and his belief in me meant the world.

Through ongoing prayer and persistence, I grabbed hold of the program given to me by the hospital and began to follow it again. I read the Bible every day, and it started to come alive to me. I was reminded that God had a plan and purpose for my life. I was alive for a reason and I must fulfill that purpose. Although anorectic thoughts and tendencies remained just a choice away, that was the one and only time I relapsed. I learned that God gives us second chances.

But we had to celebrate and be glad, because this brother of yours was dead and is alive again; he was lost and is found.

Luke 15:32

Life after Anorexia

I channeled my attention and energy back into university classes and nights and weekend science and math classes to make up the credits I did not get in my senior year of high school. I wasn't able to take the art history, painting, or sculpting classes I hoped to get because of my low GPA, and instead ended up in the only fine arts class available, drama. I hardly knew who I was; there was no way I could act in the role of someone else. I froze on stage and no words came out of my mouth. In a scene where a male actor had to kiss me, I backed away instead of leaning in. Thankfully, I was barely able to pass the course by writing a play. When I went back home to visit family on holidays, I listened to crazy, funny, true stories of what happens in hospitals as told by my mom, sister, and aunts. At some point in time, Dad told me that I "...should be a nurse, like your mom, sister and your two aunts, because then you will always have a job." I would not be a "starving artist." Doubt about my talent as an artist returned. Dad is a man of few words, but when he speaks, I listen. I was vulnerable: discouraged with university classes, continuing to struggle with low self-esteem, and desperately wanting to belong. I decided to change my pursuit of being an artist at the end of my first college year and instead begin nursing school.

I started the certified nursing assistant (CNA) program. My mom was a CNA. She said it was because she didn't believe she was smart enough to be an RN. That made me think about the medical tests done while I was in the hospital, and what I had learned about anorexia nervosa. The longer you starve your brain, the more likely you will lose gray matter or brain volume. I was bad at math, and sometimes I forgot things. Although no one told me I had brain damage, I feared that I did and that I too was not smart enough to be an RN. Drowning in self-doubt, I prayed and read the Bible daily and slowly began to realize that God created me, and He does not make junk. I also learned that if I prayed with the right motivation and intention, God would answer and guide me. I continued through the CNA program and prayerfully began the Diploma RN program. As I learned more about medicine and the self-imposed, lasting damage I might have done to my body, I left anorexia farther and farther behind me.

Despite maintaining a normal weight, I had remained amenorrheic since my periods stopped during the fall of my fifteenth year. I knew that this problem must be resolved or I would never have children. At age 21, tests showed that my ovaries were post-menopausal. In other words, non-functional. My doctor decided that as a last resort he would prescribe Clomid, a fertility drug, in an effort to shock my reproductive system into functioning again. Through side effects of flushing and headaches, eventually the medication worked, and I started having periods again. I was again reassured that God had a plan and purpose for me, and it included having a child!

God can heal. The self-imposed disease had caused my reproductive system to shut down, but God healed me. I was amazed at how much I felt alive after years of feeling dead inside, and I was even grateful for the mood swings that came with the hormonal changes. At any given time in my nursing practicum, I was crying over a sick baby, laughing in delight at a patient's lab results, or hyperventilating and passing out watching a C-section or removing a drain. There was never a dull moment.

Toby was a man in my obstetrics-gynecology rotation. He was tall, blonde, had a great sense of humor, and he wanted to date *me*. The *new* me. While I felt my body exploding with life as a result of the medication, I was afraid of the new emotions and desires I was feeling. However, I still carried around remnants of my past; I wasn't a virgin, so sex really wasn't something to cherish or value, and I certainly did not need to "save myself" for a future husband. In my mind, I believed that ship had sailed.

I ignored the thoughts that I was not attractive enough, and Toby and I began to enjoy each other. He played a big part in physically bringing me back to life. I am grateful that I was able to enjoy physical intimacy, although sometimes I could still see the inside of a tent while having sex.

Toby moved to Saudi Arabia to practice as a nurse, and I was recruited by a hospital over one thousand miles from home. Leaving all the people and places that reminded me of anorexia behind, I felt like a bird let out of my cage. God had given me a new life, and it was great! I moved and found a church, new friends, and several boyfriends. I was attracted to men who were confident, athletic, assertive, and the life of the party. I admired those qualities and wished I had them. Older, assertive men were attracted to me. I was naïve, and an easy target.

I started a second, part-time job teaching aerobics at health clubs around town and discovered the opportunity to make substantial money while doing what I loved: exercise. I spent at least an hour a day teaching and/or working out. Anorexia has lasting physical effects too. After sustaining a stress fracture of the tibia from running, breaking several toes while teaching aerobics, and breaking bones in my hand from a fall (while trail running), my bone density scan showed osteoporosis. Medications to help maintain and build bone mass were not available at that time. It was up to me to reverse it through diet, and within two years, I did. I concentrated my energy and obsessive-compulsive tendencies into ensuring that I met and exceeded the right amount of vitamins and minerals in my diet every day to rebuild bone mass. I replaced some high-impact workouts with swimming, biking, and weightlifting. People with restrictive anorexia are stubborn, determined, and persistent. As my psychiatrist had told me years before, if I channeled these traits into something positive, I would be successful.

I completed the *Eating Disorder Inventory Profile* one year after discharge from City Hospital. The assessment instrument compared my post-treatment EDI subscale scores with those of an average female college student. Significant findings were the elements of "body dissatisfaction," which was lower for me then the average female college student. I attribute this to learning acceptance of my body type and shape through counseling. My score on the element of "interpersonal distrust" was four times greater than the average female college student. I attribute this to the sexual assault that occurred when I was 15 years old, with still affected me at age 18. My "interoceptive awareness" score of 5 is significant compared to the average of 2. I believe this is due to the intense, frequent, and in-depth individual and group counseling and psychodrama while in the hospital.

The assessment instruments are completed using self-report which makes the responses variable and subject to multiple external and internal influences. If the test was completed when I was light-headed, glucose-deprived, dehydrated, under the effect of an exercise high, or in some other temporary state, self-reports will be more positive. If I was depressed, anxious, or exhausted at that time, the report would be more negative. Test takers who are not psychologically ready for help will lie and manipulate the test results. Others who are ready to accept outside help may answer the questions honestly. I saw these tests simply as part of the treatment regimen which I had accepted and surrendered to. There was no value in lying when I was trying to get better.

Do you not know that in a race all the runners run, but only one gets the prize? Run in such a way as to get the prize.

1 Corinthians 9:24 (NIV)

Accepting Jesus

Early in my 20s, I met the man who within a year would be my husband. It was a whirlwind romance with trips to Hawaii and other exciting places where a kid from the farm had never dreamed of going. The relationship moved fast, and I felt like I was riding a wave. I was sure that this was what it was "supposed to" be like; without any effort and with complete trust, the man who would be my husband would magically appear in front of me! God would place him there. We would marry, have kids, and live happily ever after. That's what happened with my mom and my sister, so I had no doubt that it would happen with me too. Despite remembering what it says in the Bible about being equally yoked, I chose to ignore it. Bruce was not a believer and did not claim to be. He told me that when he felt closest to anything that might be "god," he was in the mountains skiing or hiking. On the other hand, I had found a church and became a member. I went every week, thanking God that He had saved me.

I had this illusion in my mind, an expectation really, that I would recognize the man God had chosen for me and he would get down on one knee and ask me to marry him as we stood on a cliff in Hawaii. The latter part of my illusion happened, and I was convinced that it all had. Prayerful decision-making was not a part of deciding to marry Bruce. I believed that God had picked him out and set him in front of me to marry and live happily ever after. It was the dream of a naïve farm kid. Bruce's family had money, and I was blown away by all the money had to offer. Bruce and I dated for less than a year before getting married. It was a great year. He was a good-hearted man with a great sense of humor, but a love for alcohol. We both worked a lot of hours and developed our routines. He stopped at the bar or liquor store on the way home from work. Soon, the majority of the time when we saw one another was at night when he was drinking. This intoxicated man was not the man I loved, but he was the one I married.

I threw myself into my work and brought it home with me to be my companion through the evening. I ran and worked out. I traveled a few times a month to trade shows and presentations. Work was fun and I met a lot of people and enjoyed going to new places, but I was gone a lot. I knew that our marriage was suffering because of my travel and avoiding the problems in our marriage. However, I also knew that my travels were not the incentive for his drinking. That began a long time before he met me. I knew that I could not get to know this man at a deeper level and work on the marriage if I wasn't home. We discussed getting pregnant but I knew that wasn't a good idea. To try and save a marriage that was hanging by a thread, I took a desk job at the same company.

I learned what being married to Bruce was like on a daily basis. He had his own office in our house. In it, I would find empty beer bottles scattered around. I would clean them up and complain about it later. I stuck a pillow under my shirt to make fun of his growing beer gut. Soon, on some Saturday nights, Bruce would tell me that he was meeting a friend and would be back in a while. He would leave and return within an hour or so, and soon I learned that he was getting pot. He would smoke it in his office. I told him that I would not stop using birth control and risk getting pregnant as long as he was using drugs and drinking because I was deathly afraid that his sperm would be abnormal and we would have a child with mental or physical issues as a result. I diagnosed him (which I often and abruptly did) as an "alcoholic" and "drug addict" and insisted we go to counseling. He denied having a problem and I was frustrated. Our therapist seemed baffled and didn't know who to believe. We were in a stalemate.

One day I bought a box of clay. For weeks I molded it with no idea what it would be, only knowing that the end result would come out of my subconscious. Sculpting and carving helped me manage my stress. I lost myself in the clay for hours, and it comforted me. The sculpture ended up being a man with his head looking down and eyes closed, sitting in the palm of a very large hand, the hand of God. It served as a reminder to me that God had Bruce, and He still had me.

> He will cover you with His feathers, and under
> His wings you will find refuge; his faithfulness
> will be your shield and rampart.
>
> Psalm 91:4 (NIV)

In the midst of our marital struggles, I went on a business trip to a tradeshow out of state. As those events go, there was a lot of socializing and meeting new people. I met a tall, dark, attractive, mysterious man with a thick accent who was there representing his company. We acted professionally during the day but clearly were drawn to each other. We went out for dinner one night with a large group, and he and I stayed after they left. Over margaritas, we disclosed how unhappy we both were in our marriages. The longer we talked, the more I convinced myself that he was the only one who truly understood where I was coming from. We later ended up in my hotel room having drunk sex. I woke up early the next morning as I usually did. Through the disbelief, confusion, and nausea, I left the man in bed in my hotel room and took off running — running from my self-imposed situations and problems. He was gone by the time I returned to the hotel room, but the deep, heavy pit in my stomach was very present. I avoided him for the rest of the trade show and wondered what I would do when I got back home and faced my husband.

When I got back, I had changed, and Bruce knew it. Within a couple of days, he confronted me, asking if I had an affair. I felt worthless, ashamed, and dirty, and I denied it. The heaviness in my stomach grew into a rock. When Bruce asked me a second time a day or two later, I admitted to having the affair. I was sick with shame. I don't recall the exact timing or sequence of events, but at a later point, Bruce told me that he forgave me. Despite that, I couldn't forgive myself. I told him I wanted a divorce and impulsively left the house and moved into a cheap motel room.

I went to work during the day, usually working late into the evening, and went running before and after work. I returned to the motel room at night. For several days, I buried myself in my work and tried to figure out what to do next. I was overwhelmed with feelings of shame, guilt, humiliation, disgust, remorse, and anxiety. How could I lack self-control to the extent that I would throw away a marriage? Even worse, how could I live with myself now?

A couple of nights into my stay in the tiny ground-floor motel room, I collapsed to my knees beside the bed, crying. I felt like I had hit rock bottom again, but this time there was no way out. I knew exactly what I had done, and God would never forgive this act. I didn't know if I should be alive anymore. The self-loathing was greater than anything I had ever experienced.

At the bottom of the well of disgust and pain, I opened the drawer of the nightstand and saw the Gideon Bible. I don't know where I opened it to, but the first words I read were about forgiveness. The forgiveness of sins through Jesus' death on the cross. I realized that God gave His only son as a sacrifice to die for my sins. *Even mine. Even the sin of adultery.* I could not stop reading. I had heard the words before in church and Sunday school, but I hadn't really *heard* them. I hadn't internalized them or believed them. It was like the Bible had opened up to me for the first time and I drank in the words. Through uncontrollable sobbing, I asked Jesus into my heart that night and my life changed. I felt renewed and understood what it meant to be "born again." I understood that even the sin of adultery could be forgiven, and even I could be washed clean.

I returned to the home I shared with Bruce and started packing up my things. I knew our relationship would never be the same because of what I had done. I couldn't repair it and I was afraid that if we reconciled and tried again, when challenges arose, I would feel so guilty that anything would be permissible in order to save the marriage. Even then I realized that wasn't a healthy marriage, either. Although I was correct in knowing that I could not repair the marriage, unfortunately, I didn't understand at the time that God might have, had I asked.

I needed a place to live for a few days until I moved out, so I stayed in the house, sleeping on the couch. Bruce and I spoke, but there was no reconciliation. Within days, I filed for divorce and moved out into an apartment close to where I worked. Even with more self-induced turmoil in my life, I felt an inner peace like I had never felt before. It was the peace that comes from accepting Jesus as my personal Savior. I knew that even *I* had been forgiven and my sins had been washed away. Because of that, I could carry on. I was reminded that I was here for a reason, otherwise the anorexia would have taken my life, or I would have taken it myself in that motel room. God wanted me here, and He still had a lot of work for me to do. So, I moved forward. Similar to the slow suicide of anorexia nervosa, the guilt, shame, and remorse of sin can take a person to the point of suicide.

I left this situation with the definite and defiant knowledge that I would never, ever put myself in that place again; I would never commit adultery again. God loved me so much that He had pulled me from the depths of despair and death a second time, and because of Jesus, even I was forgiven. Jesus instructed me to leave my life of sin and choose a different path, and I thank God for a chance to do that. We cannot give what we do not have. Because I was forgiven, I was able to forgive others: the bus driver, the man in the tent, even my aunt.

> Jesus straightened up and asked her, "Woman, where are they? Has no one condemned you?" "No one, sir," she said. "Then neither do I condemn you," Jesus declared. "Go now and leave your life of sin."
>
> John 8:10-11 (NIV)

Red Flags

I picked up the pieces and moved forward, dragging the memories of a divorce behind me. Within a few short years I met another man at an athletic club party. He was similar to my first husband in that he had an entertaining, albeit quirky, sense of humor. He was street smart with a sordid past and "bad-boy" aura that I found extremely attractive and exciting. He came to church with me on occasion; a "Creaster" (Christmas and Easter) type of guy, but I put the same blinders on and chose not to see that as a problem.

    I jumped into the relationship with both feet, relying on blind faith, trust, and optimism, again. I wasn't sure what happened the last time, but I tried to put it behind me, and thought THIS surely had to be the man God had chosen for me! We got engaged, I sold my condo, and I moved in with him. I chose to ignore red flags: controlling, angry behavior, lies, and self-centeredness. I blindly participated in his deceitful efforts, including insurance fraud. I bought a high-end road bike; together we trained for long road bike rides.

    Five months after getting the bike, I was going too fast downhill on a winding road, and to avoid hitting an oncoming vehicle, I intentionally went down on pavement. With no broken bones but leaving part of my right butt cheek on the pavement, I limped home to patch myself up. A week later, I did a similar ride despite being exhausted and bandaged up from the earlier accident. This time I hit a German shepherd on the downhill. I did an endo and landed on the pavement on my head and right shoulder. I was unconscious for a time and sustained a fractured clavicle and scapula, broken helmet, and concussion.

When my fiancé took me home from the ED, I had sprained thumbs and back pain. Road rash sheared the entire right side of my body, my right arm was in a sling, and I was wrapped in bandages. The next few weeks were foggy. I needed help with many things: bathing, brushing my hair and teeth, getting food and drink, and opening doors. My sudden dependence on him revealed my fiancé's true colors. He now was able to control if, when, and how I did almost everything, because I needed help with almost everything. I stood naked and shivering in the claw foot bathtub, waiting as time passed before he would decide he had finished breakfast and could help me step out. He entertained his ex-girlfriend in our house while I slept and tried to recover. Through the brain fog, I thought I saw red flags but felt helpless to do anything about them. I needed his help. Three months later, I tried to forget what I thought I had seen, and we were married.

The words that doctors had told me in the hospital resounded in my head; my ovaries were postmenopausal. Even though I was ovulating without medication at this point, doctors had explained that it was "very unlikely" that I would ever be able to have children. In my early 30s, I knew it had to be now or never. Both my husband and I wanted a child. There was nothing I wanted in life more. I read everything I could get my hands on to learn what to do to increase the chances of getting pregnant. I knew that although anorexia was a memory, getting pregnant and having a child was another way to psychologically overcome the disease.

I created and followed ovulation charts and learned what could improve my chances, carefully monitoring and recording all factors on a daily basis. Within four months, I was pregnant! I turned my attention to the pregnancy and learned all I could about what it takes to have a healthy baby. During that period of time, my husband was away from home more and not mentally present when he was around. As I turned my attention inward to the life growing inside me, he turned his outward, enjoying dive and surfing trips with other people. I knew we were drifting apart and came to understand that our marriage was built on a common interest alone: athletics. There was nothing deeper than that; the roots were shallow.

Although I kept working out, it was within the limits set by my obstetrician. I had a human being growing inside me and that was far more important than my own compulsive exercising behavior. Despite the nagging concern about my husband pulling away, I was thrilled with the new life inside of me and thanked God many times every day for the precious gift He had entrusted me with. Our child was born on his due date, healthy and beautiful. That was indeed the best day of my life. He was a content, easy baby and I loved spending every minute with him. At the same time, my husband drifted, we argued, and within three years, our shallow marriage crumbled in fear and anger.

The divorce was long, painful and expensive. Our three-year-old was assigned joint parenting time. Even through the trials, the unknown, a broken heart, another broken relationship, seeing nothing ahead but an escape from the present, feeling an overwhelming sense of responsibility to parent a precious child, I still felt God's presence. As in struggles before, at my lowest point, I would pick up my Bible and just start reading. God gave his son, Jesus, to die for my sins, even mine. I had been entrusted with the most precious gift of a human being. I knew that parenting this boy was part of the purpose God had for me, and I focused all of my attention and resources on him. Parenting changes a person. I knew that I needed help and asked God to stand in as his Father. I knew He accepted.

Satan strikes where we are weakest, and in my case that is with anxiety and worry. Our son went back and forth in a structured parenting program until age 16. For much of the first three years after the divorce, my anxiety controlled me. I worried about our son's safety, sleep, well-being, what he ate and drank, where he was, car accidents, and whatever other worry entered my mind. At some point in time, the anxiety controlled me, and I started having physical symptoms of stomach pain and headaches. I was numb to everything else around me, except my son.

It was at that time a wise, close friend suggested that I see a counselor, so I did. Through counseling, I was reminded to pray, and able to yield my worry to God. As soon as I would surrender it, He would lift it away from me. I knew that God was with my child when I was not. God was protecting him. I knew that God had big plans for him and would protect him from all harm, and I was able to rest in that knowledge. However, human nature is such that we forget, and waves of worry would flood over me again. Then I would again remember God's presence, and surrender the anxiety. God would swiftly take it from me, and I would relax and be able to make it through the next few days. The cycle continued for three years. It took me three years to understand that God is always present and He would never leave or forsake us. If we surrender, He is always ready and able to meet our needs. Once the weight was truly lifted, I knew I could carry on with life. I knew that letting go and letting God take over would make me a better parent. Our son was safely cradled in God's hands.

> Cast all your anxiety on Him because He cares for you.
>
> 1 Peter 5:7

The next few years were filled with child-raising, job changes, advancing my education, and several more dysfunctional, broken relationships. I have read that first-time victims become repeat victims and I believe it. For me, risky sexual behavior was set at a higher bar, and I took risks after the sexual assault that would not have been taken otherwise. Predators can quickly spot potential victims. One such experience began innocently at the neighborhood coffee shop.

When my son was about 6 years old, we left the house early on a weekday before school and work to get breakfast at the coffee shop. That morning as we sat and enjoyed breakfast, I noticed a man watching us. He looked over and smiled a few times and then turned back to the women he was sitting with. I thought nothing of it until after we left and were driving on the highway. A truck pulled beside me, horn honking. I looked over, annoyed at crazy drivers everywhere, to see that it was the man from the coffee shop. He was motioning for me to pull over.

I frantically looked around to see if I had left my purse in the coffee shop or on the roof of the car (which would not have been the first time). I exited the highway at the next opportunity and pulled into a gas station. The man in the truck pulled in behind me. I stepped out of the car and he met me, grinning widely and carrying a football. He explained that he felt "drawn" to me and my son in the coffee shop. He wanted to give the football to my son as a gift. The football was new and was signed "Troy" with a black sharpie. Troy explained that he was a well-known former college football player. I was delighted that he had taken an interest in us, although the feeling in my stomach warned me that this scenario was rather unusual. As I often did, I chose to ignore that feeling, thanked him, and accepted the gift. My son was happy with it and clutched it all the way to school. Troy had also given me a business card with his name and the name of an insurance company where he worked. He asked me to give him a call because he would like to see us again. I knew little about football, especially college football, and wouldn't have recognized a player's name or the player himself if he were standing right in front of me. I didn't take the time to research who this man claimed to be.

After waiting the obligatory two days, I called him. We agreed to meet, and the first date led to a second. Within a couple of weeks, Troy was offering to help with birthday party arrangements for my son, and I agreed. Our relationship grew physical very fast. He was a very attractive man with a strong athletic body that he obviously took very good care of. He wore trendy, expensive clothes and had an outgoing, charismatic way about him. Physical attraction towards him shrouded the questions I had about why he frequently didn't answer his phone and often canceled dates at the last minute. As per my usual practice, I paid attention to only what I wanted to see, not seeing the red flags. Troy and I planned to spend Thanksgiving weekend together. My son was to be at his dad's house for the holiday break. We planned to go out several places and meet his family. Troy suddenly stopped calling me two days before the holiday, and Thanksgiving Day came and went without contact. Besides the disappointment, I had a burning pit in my stomach warning me that there was a problem here.

I left several voice messages for him, and he called me the morning after Thanksgiving. Troy solemnly informed me that his aunt and uncle had been killed in a head-on car crash two days before. He was calling from Kansas City where they and most of his family lived. He explained that his aunt and uncle had raised him because his parents were uninvolved in his life. He had been very close to them, and he was in shock. He cried over the phone, and I did my best to console him, even offering to catch a flight and meet him to offer support. He declined my offer but continued to call me several more times that day and through the next, updating me on funeral planning and family gatherings. I listened, trying to be supportive and helpful.

When we spoke on the phone, I could hear the voices of men and women in the background. A woman who claimed to be Troy's sister spoke briefly to me, and I told her I was sorry for their loss. The funeral was to be held on Monday. During a phone call late Saturday night, Troy tearfully told me that he, as the oldest sibling, was responsible for buying the caskets for his aunt and uncle. He explained that they were very expensive and since he didn't get paid until the following week, he didn't have enough money to pay for them. My heart went out to him. I had worked hard to save three thousand dollars over the past year and had it as my only savings in an account. I offered the money to Troy as a loan. He sobbed into the phone as he graciously accepted the offer and thanked me profusely many times over. He reassured me that he would promptly pay me back when he got paid the following week, and I agreed.

Troy suggested I send the three thousand dollars via MoneyGram, which is a person-to-person funds transfer from a location such as Walmart. I agreed, but again offered to fly there to attend the funeral with him and bring the cash at that time. He declined, thanking me again for that offer. As soon as I could arrange it, I drove 15 minutes to the nearest Walmart and sent the money. It was very fast and easy to send. Within minutes after sending it, Troy called to thank me. That was the last call he made to me. I called his number and left several messages on his voice mail over the next few days. Monday came and went, and then Tuesday and Wednesday. Life continued as it was with work and school, but I grew more and more anxious as time passed.

I kept telling myself, "If that were me, I'd be so wrapped up I wouldn't take the time to call anyone outside of immediate family." So, in my usual fashion, I gave him the benefit of the doubt and more time. However, the nagging feeling that this was not right remained. On Thursday, I decided to go back to the place where I had sent the money from. I asked the representative at the MoneyGram desk if he could track where and to whom the money had been sent. He did. It had been sent only five miles from my current location. My heart raced and I felt like I would faint. I told the guy at the MoneyGram desk that I had been conned for 3K. He politely explained that he could do nothing, and if this were true, I should call the police.

First, I called Troy and asked him how he could live with himself after this lie, how he could screw over someone who was generous and trusting enough to wire him 3K, and how he could use my son to manipulate me. He never picked up, so I left message after message, some crying, some yelling, but most repeating my disbelief, until his voice mail was full. After work that day, I picked up my son and headed to the police station to file a theft report. While my child played on his Gameboy, I wrote a police report and spoke to an officer about what had happened. He took Troy's phone number and called him with me listening. Troy must have seen that the PD was calling, because he immediately picked up the phone. After the officer explained why he was calling, Troy described the same story he had told me, insisting that the money was a loan, which he fully intended to pay back. The officer hung up the phone and advised me to file the report, but because it was "a loan," to wait for Troy to pay me back. I got the impression that he thought I was over-reacting, and everything would be fine if I would just relax and be patient.

I was crushed, knowing full well that I had emptied my savings account and there was no way in hell I would ever be paid back. I blamed myself and my naiveté. That's what you get for being a dumb farm kid in the city and trusting people; you can take the kid from the farm, but you can't take the farm from the kid, even decades later. I wrestled with myself for days, even calling Troy several times more, crying and asking for the money. I was furious and haunted the coffee shop where I first saw him, knowing that if by chance he were walking and I were driving, I would hit him with my car. My anger was frightening, even to me. I felt frustrated, betrayed, and used, and it was eating me up inside. The anxiety I often carried about not having any money in a savings account in case of an emergency was back in full force and I was furious that I had willingly given it to a thief.

Unable to concentrate on work or anything else, and just barely functioning as a parent and employee, I finally remembered where to find help. After church on Sunday, the elders stood at the front of the sanctuary and asked anyone who was struggling to come forward. I was, so I went. I shared the story of Troy with an older woman who listened with sympathy and no judgement. I cried and she comforted me; we prayed that God would lift this anguish from me and allow me to move past it. She reminded me that God can make good things out of bad, and that He would in this case. She said that we don't know enough to judge. Yes, Troy stole the money, but that was not the question. Was there a higher purpose? Did he need it to have the basic necessities of food

Red Flags

and shelter? We didn't know. All we knew was that "In all things God works for the good of those who love Him..." We could rest in that knowledge.

I left the church feeling overwhelmed and spent. I would like to say that I immediately felt at peace, but I didn't. It took a few days and more voice messages to Troy, which were never returned. I even spoke with an attorney and a private investigator to learn what, if any options I had to get the money back. Every option would cost me more money, and it was extremely unlikely that I would ever get the money back from Troy.

One morning I woke up and knew that I had finally let God lift the burden from me. I felt a peace beyond understanding and was able to carry on with life.

As He always had, God provided for us financially. We always had enough. Over a year later, there was an envelope in the mail from MoneyGram. Like most of my mail, I thought it was junk and almost filed it in the garbage, but on second thought opened it. It was a reimbursement check for $2,800.00 as a result of a lawsuit filed against MoneyGram. THAT is God in action!

> And we know in all things God works for
> the good of those who love Him, who have
> been called according to His purpose.
>
> Romans 8:28 (NIV)

Double A

I try not to, but I think about what it was like to lie on the operating table in the OR right before they removed my breasts. How vulnerable I was. How open and unprotected. Just like I feel having this book published. I hope that something in these words and experiences will resonate with you, give you comfort, and inspire you to tell your own story.

One gal I know who also had a bilateral mastectomy described the surgery as being "filleted." Like a fish. A fish is pulled out of the protective environment and then flops around, struggling to breathe. Then, before it knows what happened, it is filleted open. Pulled out of my usual predictable and protected environment, the fear of impending surgery, then, the fillet.

I saw a movie a couple of weeks before my mastectomy surgery. The setting was in Africa or something. There is infighting with brutality and mutilation between armed men and civilians. I cannot recall the name of the movie or anything else about it, except when it showed a woman who had recently given birth. She had been breastfeeding. The men cut her breasts off, and she lay there with arms spread wide, slowly bleeding to death. Watching her shiver as she went into shock, the person who finally found her gave her a sedative. It relaxed her and she died. For several nights before mastectomy surgery, I had that image in my head and my pulse would race in terror. I finally prayed that God would lift that image from my mind, which he did at once, and he kept it away.

When I received the email from my surgeon's office to confirm the second surgery (reconstruction), my stomach knotted in a now familiar way. I was reminded of being unable to sit up in bed by myself, and when I tried to anyway, the sharp pain in my chest took my breath away. I remembered having to sleep on my back and how sore my lower back and butt got after lying that way for hours.

As a divorced mom of a 16-year-old boy, I felt a lot of responsibility. I was in the third year of my third marriage at the time, and it was not going well. The frequency of my husband's mood swings was back to where they originally were, almost every week. Even without the Master's degree in psychology that I had just attained, anyone would agree that there was something very wrong with him. Regular people do not fly into a rage, kicking chairs, throwing things, hitting furniture, and jumping up and down naked while slapping their own head when they are anxious, or something doesn't go their way. The episodes of rage would occur at 10 p.m. or later, and usually involved frustration over sex; not getting it enough or in the way he wanted, or telling me that I didn't seem "into it."

My natural response to the rage was to shut down. I would sit or lie there, waiting for it to end. This was not the response he wanted, so the rage escalated to the point of him repeatedly slamming his fist into his other hand an inch from my face. I tried yelling back at him once but discovered that it only escalated his rage to a frightening level. Then one night I just sank to my knees beside our bed and closed my eyes, clasped my hands together in prayer. All I could pray was, "God help me," over and over again. In this posture, God heard my prayer. Instantly, my husband got dressed and left the house, slamming doors as he went. He probably drove to the -all-night gym to work out, as he sometimes did. After a while, I fell into a deep, grateful sleep, knowing that God had provided a way for me to get through the experience the next time and the time after that. God doesn't prevent these bad things from happening, but he does create a way through them.

In the middle of this, I followed up on an abnormal mammogram and was diagnosed with breast cancer. How could someone with a double-A cup size even GET breast cancer? There is no breast tissue there to get cancer in! I had no known risk factors; no smoking, I had given birth and breastfed a child, my diet was clean, and I exercised like a fiend and was not overweight. Yet, I had developed 12 areas of early cancer in my right breast over the course of one year. I learned that although I thought I was doing everything perfectly to prevent cancer and essentially was invincible, cancer didn't think so. Cancer doesn't play favorites. Cancer didn't think I was so unique, perfect, or so much better than everyone else. I was humbled by that knowledge and cut down a few notches. I wasn't so great after all.

When I told my husband the diagnosis, he proceeded to tell me not to interrupt him as he described his chiropractic visit of the day. When he was done describing the details of his chiropractic visit, he asked me what I said; "Something about cancer?" I felt defeated and exhausted, so I just told him "I have breast cancer," and I went to sleep.

During the next few weeks, it became apparent that he was unable to support me. I had gone from a strong, independent woman to a dependent woman desperately in need of support and comfort. He was not in the business of comforting, so I made the decision to go it alone with the support of my son and family. The decision to do a bilateral mastectomy was made based on the fact that I needed to do whatever it took to eliminate the cancer forever. I was reminded of the anorexia treatment and the choice I made to go "all in." I knew that also in this situation going all in wasn't my only choice, but it would be my choice. Breasts were made for a purpose and mine had served their purpose in nourishing a child for a year. My 16-year-old son still needed his mom in other ways, and God still has more work for me to do here.

I had the option of reconstructive surgery. With a history of anorexia still lurking like a small devil creature in the back of my mind, I pictured myself as the prepubescent girl with anorexia 25 years earlier and debated that outcome. Ironically, I remembered the self-hypnosis for breast enlargement that Dr. Thomas had tried to teach me (which by the way, didn't work), and attending a seminar on breast enhancement surgery in my early 20s (which I couldn't afford, even with a nurses' discount). I had even shopped in a lingerie store for breast cancer survivors, but I thought the padding looked just like that — padding. I had put the idea of having even normal-sized breasts out of my mind until now. I had to smile, thinking that God has a great sense of humor and can make a way when there is no way, so I elected for reconstructive surgery.

The surgeon was a bright man my age, full of energy and life. He had 20 years of experience with people with my diagnosis, and at my first appointment he asked me, "What breast size have you always wanted to be?" His question made me feel confused. I told him I didn't know. He looked a little confused himself. I asked him what he recommended, since he had done this for so many years, and he advised "big B, small C." So, that's what I did. There were no complications and I emerged from mastectomy surgery with expanders under my skin, creating larger breasts than when I went in!

My mom, dad, and my child helped me get through a few weeks postop when I could not use my arms for much, and I filed for divorce. Over the next few months, the tissue expanders were filled once a week with solution to stretch the skin and prepare for implants. It was an uncomfortable time, but I never doubted the decision. It was another step taken to leave anorexia and small breasts in my past. The reconstructive surgery went well, but I had a lot to get used to. For several months, I stayed home as much as possible, trying to adjust to the new me. The divorce and moving to a new house distracted me. I spent my time at physical therapy, redeveloping upper body strength, endurance, and flexibility, and trying to reach a point where I felt a bit like myself again.

At a post-op visit with my surgeon, he announced that my breasts looked "fricking incredible!" I looked at him like he was from some other planet, and while I felt flattered, I also knew his opinion was biased. Several months passed in solitude, functioning as a mom and working at home as I tried to accept my new, strange breasts. I was afraid to hug my son or go outside in only one layer of clothing, for fear everyone knew, and they were strange to everyone else too.

Finally, over a year later, I called a trusted old friend. He was a man I had dated on and off between divorces. A kind, loving, humble, and understanding man; in those ways, nothing like my three ex-husbands. I invited him over on a night when I was alone in the house, and at an intimate moment, he simply said that my breasts "look normal." I didn't even know what I needed to hear, but he said it. I just wanted to finally be normal. I could move forward. I am forever grateful to him for what he said to me that night.

The Lord himself goes before you and will be with you; he will never leave you nor forsake you. Do not be afraid; do not be discouraged.

Deuteronomy 31:8 (NIV)

Analysis

The Psychology of Anorexia

Anorexia nervosa has been called slow suicide. Statistics are fluid, but the mortality rate for anorexia nervosa remains the highest of all psychiatric illnesses. Around 20 percent of people die from it, with 5 percent dying within 10 years of being diagnosed. In close to half of all deaths, suicide is the cause. Other causes of death are complications of the disorder including cardiac abnormality and electrolyte imbalance. In people with eating disorders, some statistics claim that suicide rates are 18 times that of the general population. One-quarter to one-half of people with anorexia nervosa practice non-suicidal self-injury such as cutting, hitting, and scratching. Theoretically, they feel that they don't belong anywhere and are a burden to people who love them. They have a higher than normal physical pain threshold, and greater capacity to accept pain as a result of repeated exposure to it. These factors increase the likelihood of suicide attempts.

Back in the 1980s, anorexia nervosa was even more enigmatic than it is now. It was associated with moral deficits such as narcissism, perfectionism, and vanity. Research has shown that people with anorexia have a need to conform, are people pleasers, and have low self-esteem. Unlike other psychiatric disorders such as depression or bipolar disorder, which are associated with serious psychosis, dangerousness, homelessness, and poverty, people instead want to be thin, making eating disordered behavior desirable. Eating disorders are often glamorized. What adolescent girl didn't want to look like the skinny models in designer clothing? I had support from family and others who knew me before anorexia and seemed to understand the self-imposed suffering. However, I also heard many random comments from others who supported my waif-like appearance. They told me I was "so lucky" to be thin. They asked me how I did it because they wanted to be thin as well. Early in anorexia I relished those comments, but as the disease took over my life, even I thought those people were crazy.

People with anorexia are not only afraid of being fat, but also of being ordinary, average, or plain. Early in the disease when the attention from others increases, people with anorexia will continue doing whatever it takes to stand out, even to the point of self-starvation. There is a turning point when I reached a weight that no longer looked desirable to the majority of people. I looked sick and started hearing comments such as, "Do you have cancer?" or, "Do you have AIDS?" At that point, anorexia was gaining strength and I was losing myself to the disease.

Inborn personality traits that maintain anorexia include being shy, introverted, rigid, and excessively detail-oriented. People with anorexia have trouble seeing the "big picture,' or changing from one task to another, and crave predictability. They are anxious perfectionists with a propensity to avoid emotional experiences, likely because of our own difficulty recognizing, regulating, and expressing emotions. Over time, they believe that these traits help manage stress and cope with day-to-day challenges. Like other mental health disorders where drinking, sex, drugs, violence, hoarding, or hair plucking are used as coping strategies, false beliefs make treatment challenging. The beliefs are present at an early age (even before anorexia), flourish with active disease, and often remain, albeit in muted form, years to decades after recovery.

Anorexia nervosa is characterized by self-imposed diet and behavior strategies with the goals of losing weight and self-punishment. Over time, maladaptive patterns of eating take on a life of their own. Exercise, at times to the point of collapse, is used not only to manage stress, but also to distract from feelings of hunger.

People with anorexia often feel alone. In the depths of the disease, they feel as though no one understands their personal torment. People with anorexia lack the ability to identify their own feelings or understand their wants and needs. They feel guilty to even want or need anything. They cannot ask for what they want or need, but expect other people to know. Treatment that includes self-awareness and personal empowerment strengthens their self-confidence, and helps them realize that they have to ask for what they need. Self-esteem also gradually relieves feelings of guilt. The person with anorexia must be reminded that no one can read their mind. The only way to have unspoken needs or wants fulfilled is with luck.

Factors that increase the likelihood of body-image disorders include a history of being teased, parent and peer modeling, social focus on body weight, parental prompting to control weight, and sexual assault or abuse. Body image has been described as elastic, improving and worsening based on internal and external influences. The media portrayal of thin as beautiful and comments from others affected how I felt about myself in real-time, but self-loathing was always the baseline.

Distorted body image is a central feature of eating disorders. It is an altered perception of and preoccupation with overall body mass. Individuals with eating disorders may also be preoccupied with certain body parts such as thighs or stomach, fitting the description of body dysmorphic disorder, but because the overwhelming concern is about body mass, distorted body image is predominant. When I looked in the mirror, I was simply dissatisfied with everything from the top of my head to the tip of my toes. I didn't always or necessarily see a fat person in the mirror, but I did see all the ways my appearance could be improved. Early in anorexia, I was very proud of how I looked, but as my weight got lower and lower, pride was replaced by dissatisfaction and even disgust. I went from wearing form-fitting, skin-showing clothing, to covering up my body and trying to find loose clothes that simply weren't painful to wear. I was so cold most of the time that getting warm became my priority. Underlying depression sustains body dissatisfaction. Negative parental or peer modeling of weight concerns contributes to body dissatisfaction. The more depression and greater body dissatisfaction, the more eating disorder symptoms progress.

Many people with anorexia love to prepare and serve food to others. They enjoy it through someone else, minus the calories. Preparing rich, satisfying meals but not eating them might be a subconscious demonstration of complete control over eating. Early in the disorder, I loved to watch people eat high-calorie, high-fat food as this supported my vanity. ("I could refuse that food while others could not.") Later on, as preoccupation with food and eating became commonplace, I would smell and see the food that I would deny myself, and feel hunger pains and hear my stomach growling. I would crave it but often would not allow myself to eat it. Poor self-esteem and body dissatisfaction stood in my way. If I was unable to resist, I would try to satisfy the craving and hunger with low-calorie foods. Sometimes it worked and sometimes it didn't. As many people with eating disorders do (under-eaters and over-eaters alike), I would offer to clean up after meals, and in that time frame eat small bits of leftovers when I thought no one was watching. How sad.

Feelings of obligation and responsibility and the pursuit of perfection will leave you disappointed. People with anorexia cannot possibly achieve all the goals they set for themselves. The bar is set to an unattainable height. Inability to achieve my own goals set me up for dysfunctional behavior. No matter what I did, I could never reach my own goals. I wanted to be the fastest runner, have the best boyfriend, and wear the nicest, trendiest clothes. I wanted to be the most popular girl in my class. I wanted everyone to like me and to wish they were like me. My pursuit went too far, ultimately doing the opposite and turning everyone away. When that happened, I tried even harder; losing more weight and exercising more, until anorexia controlled me. Under its control and believing I was helpless, I embraced being different and odd, and pursued perfection in that. I wanted to be unique. It didn't matter how, even if it killed me. Don't let the pursuit of perfection ruin your life.

The course of anorexia nervosa varies. It can be a single episode with recovery, a waxing and waning course over time, or a chronic and worsening trajectory. It can transition to bingeing, purging, and bulimia, or even to "drunkorexia," which is a form of bulimia. It is drinking alcohol in lieu of eating, which results in a rapid high without ingesting many calories. It can lead to cardiac arrhythmias, disordered sleep, and poor general health. The goal of maintaining a slim-appearing physique can cost everything. This pattern is easy to fall into, easy to overlook, and extremely complicated to overcome. If this is you, you can overcome this. This deadly lifestyle can be reversed. It does not have to control you. We have all made poor choices, but God is our creator, and He understands. First, admit that you have messed up, and ask for forgiveness. Then surrender your problem to your creator; ask God for help. He will place the right people in the right places for you, because He loves you. Get professional help from a dietitian. Change your daily routine; get up earlier, go to bed earlier. Remove the alcohol and drink something else. Drunkorexia is similar to bulimia except that alcohol is the substance used for bingeing.

> Jesus went through Galilee, teaching in their synagogues, proclaiming the good news of the kingdom, and healing every disease and sickness among the people.
>
> Matthew 4:23 (NIV)

Comorbidities and Triggers

Just like hypertension goes with heart disease, a mental health condition is rarely seen in isolation. Mental health conditions often overlap, with some more pervasive than others. Common comorbid disorders seen with anorexia nervosa include anxiety, depression, or obsessive-compulsive disorder.

Three-quarters of people with anorexia report depression, and 25 percent report one or more anxiety disorders (such as phobias) that persist for decades after recovery. Obsessive-compulsive disorder is seen in up to 30 percent of people who have recovered. Up to 80 percent have obsessions and/or compulsive behavior. Alcohol and substance use disorders occur in up to 25 percent, but are less likely to occur in people who had restricting anorexia because of fear of losing control and/or consuming too many calories.

Fear is present tense, like when you are chased by a badger. Anxiety is future tense, anxiety about what could happen. Anorexia nervosa is characterized by both fear and anxiety. People with anorexia have an overwhelming, real-time fear of failure or rejection. Their goal is nothing less than perfection, so failure is always lying in wait. They believe that acceptance is based on outward appearance. Being "slim" is acceptable. With anything else, rejection is inevitable. Anxiety is focused on the next meal, the next hour, or the next interaction with someone.

People with anorexia also tend to use their anxiety

as leverage. Anxiety can be a reason not to eat. Allowing anxiety to take control of the mind can decrease or even eliminate feelings of hunger. It is a believable reason not to eat, and people with anorexia are never at a loss for great (or any) reasons not to eat. Ironically, for some people anxiety is a reason to overeat or drink too much. Either way it's the same; we are all looking for a way to manage anxiety, and gain some semblance of control.

Along with depression and anxiety, focused obsessive-compulsive disorder often coincides with anorexia nervosa. Instead of the more common obsession with germs and compulsive hand-washing, people with anorexia are obsessed with food, drink, and weight. Their obsessions are revealed in compulsive, ritualistic behavior including counting and limiting the number of food items, and prohibiting different food items to touch one another on the plate. People with anorexia nervosa only use special dishware. Frantic cleaning, excessive exercise, frequent weight checks, and other warped behaviors are practiced with the pathetic intent to relieve anxiety and feel in control. Even post-recovery, the behaviors may continue, or be limited to only those that do not draw as much attention.

Cause and effect are blurred in anorexia nervosa; does starvation cause the psychological symptoms, or does the mind drive a person to self-imposed starvation? In my opinion, they feed off of each other (no pun intended). As I lost more weight, the psychological symptoms worsened. As they worsened, my self-esteem decreased, and distorted eating behaviors increased, so I lost more weight. Reason ultimately flew out the window and destructive habits became more ingrained, so I lost more weight. Anorexia nervosa is a vicious, circular battle of the mind.

When groundwork is already laid, sexual abuse or assault can trigger an eating disorder, arouse a latent eating disorder, or intensify an existing eating disorder. Thereafter, a similar experience, event, or circumstance triggers body-image distress and disordered eating behavior. Until a person with anorexia understands the cause and effect, anorectic tendencies will continue and even be lifelong. It took me many years and many hours of counseling to truly understand and believe that what happened to me was not my fault. That being said, it took decades to get to a place where I forgave the people involved. I had to learn that that forgiveness was not for them; it was for me. In fact, the person you forgive doesn't even need to know you forgive them. Forgiveness lifts the weight off of you so that you can live.

Eating disorder behaviors are learned, practiced, and habitual. Triggers are often emotional and include anger, depression, anxiety, boredom, or feelings of helplessness. Just like every other addiction, it's important to see triggers for what they are, and then plan how to react. Hunger and negative feelings increase the likelihood of bingeing. A person with bulimia copes by bingeing and purging. A person with anorexia will restrict eating and drinking, and exercise to exhaustion. Disordered eating can be perceived as a coping mechanism gone wrong. Whatever the behavioral response, once you learn that it relieves the emotion, albeit temporarily, it will continue as the primary coping mechanism until it is replaced with something else.

A person with anorexia must explore their past. We cannot change the past or control the present or future, but in understanding our past we can change how we react now. Choose a healthy, positive replacement for the usual dysfunctional response, and use it without delay. Practicing this the first time is terrifying. In times of fear or anxiety, I replaced excessive exercise and not eating with reading and prayer. I practiced this over and over until I trusted that it would work, and the replacement became a habit. Do not choose or use a person to replace a practice. People will disappoint you; a person won't always be there when you need him to be, or in the way you want him to be simply because that person is not a mind reader. It is so important to learn about yourself and choose a reliable, personal replacement that you have immediate access to. Map out the days and weeks ahead to see where you will need to use your new coping strategy. Forecast times of struggle and be positive and confident about how you will cope when that time arrives. Feelings of helplessness and hopelessness trigger destructive habits, up to and including deliberate self-harm. Obsessive exercise, cutting, burning, picking, and causing physical pain arises from a place of deep despair. Avoid that place.

Self-imposed food restrictions are a means of gaining control. The stock market is falling, credit card bills are growing, the country is divided, and we are in a pandemic. The person with anorexia thinks, "The world is out of my control, but my body is not. I can control what I eat. See how well I can do that? On the outside you will see that I am completely in control, but you do not know what is going on inside me. I am overwhelmed with anxiety about the past, present, future, and everything that I cannot control, so I will control what I can control, what I eat." The enemy finds ways to be invisible and anywhere. With anorexia, the enemy is in the mind. With cancer, the enemy is in the body. With coronavirus, the enemy is in the air. So then, what can we do? Know that God is more powerful than any enemy, whether inside or outside.

I am the gate; whoever enters through me will be saved. They will come in and go out, and find pasture. The thief comes only to steal and kill and destroy; I have come that they may have life, and have it to the full."

John 10: 9-11 NIV

Coercion and Compulsion

Forcibly hospitalizing a person with anorexia should be a last resort. Learning about the disease and treatment options, and one-to-one counseling were steps that led me to a place where I asked God for help. Just like smoking or drug and alcohol abuse, learning about the harm you are doing to your body, and trying to stop are steps that lead to lasting recovery. Even if you have tried to stop and failed time and time again, don't give up on yourself.

Coercion (using threats to force a person to do something they otherwise would not do) and compulsion (elimination of choice or freedom) are often used in the treatment of anorexia nervosa. Most who are or have recovered agree that there can be value in using coercion and/or compulsion. Compulsion is often thought to be by legal means per the Mental Health Act of 1983 and enforced if the patient is a risk to themselves or others. Unless the person with anorexia is so weak that they cannot resist, or they have decided to accept help, voluntary treatment is unlikely.

Forced treatment often results in the person with anorexia responding with equal and opposite force. In this case, they may get worse instead of better. Threatening to use legal means to enforce treatment, or leveraging parental consent for a minor can be acceptable ways to use compulsion when the person with anorexia refuses treatment, even though death is imminent.

Coercion is frequently used to enforce treatment and can be perceived as useful or manipulative. Anorexia patients are hypervigilant of the stares and comments of others. Paranoia and distrust can result in the perception of coercion even when it is not being used.

Medical causes of death in anorexia include heart failure, pulmonary edema, or respiratory failure. The majority of people with anorexia at any stage of the disease agree that no one should be allowed to die as a result of a self-imposed and treatable illness. Regardless of the type of coercion or compulsive measure used to enforce treatment, retrospective analysis by people with anorexia who have recovered agree that it was appropriate and ethical, even if they were reluctant to accept or blatantly objected to it at the time. Just like a child, due to medical and psychological factors, the person with anorexia may not know what's good for her.

People with anorexia may resist treatment because they perceive the disease as their identity. They are afraid of what may happen if they let it go. Loss of control is another reason why they resist treatment. The real-time, short and long-term effects of anorexia negatively impact cognition. People with anorexia lose reasonable judgement and are unable to understand the dangers of the disease, or they are simply too exhausted and depressed to care.

Inability to concentrate and poor reasoning is a result of progressive malnutrition. Similar to people who have dementia, people with anorexia are less able to recall, process, or store information. The starving brain simply cannot learn or remember. Hypoglycemia is common and often ongoing with moderate to severe anorexia nervosa. Select studies show that long-term hypoglycemia causes brain atrophy. Altered hormone levels including decreased estrogen, oxytocin, testosterone and leptin and high cortisol contribute to decreased cognition and mood disorders including depression, anxiety, and disordered eating behavior. Decreased neurotransmitters including serotonin and dopamine add to these symptoms. The detrimental effects on moods and cognition must be considered when attempting to convince patients of the need for treatment. They may be incapable of reasoning or understanding that immediate treatment is necessary to save their life. Depression can make people with anorexia so apathetic that they simply don't care.

Sometimes people with anorexia know they need help, but other times they do not. They want a way out of anorexia, but also do not. If they are not ready to surrender the disease, nothing anyone says or does will be effective. People with anorexia need to be told that they no longer control the disease, the disease is controlling them. A person overcome with this disease is not able to change unless they decide that it's time to give up the disease. It is like releasing a demon that is in control of your life, much the same as addiction to alcohol, drugs, gambling, sex or gaming. The addiction is in control, and it takes enormous effort to release it. Once released, it can reemerge at any point in time if the person allows it. In my case, I knew without a doubt that if I truly asked God for help and surrendered the disease to Him, He would help me. I chose not to ask for help until I hit bottom. When will you finally hit the bottom? Before it happens, I implore you to look up, because your help is right there waiting. Confess your sins, surrender the disease, and ask for help.

Connections with others are important when making treatment decisions. Coercion and even compulsory treatment methods can be acceptable in the presence of a trusting relationship between the treating provider and the person with anorexia. In the case of parents and other family members, a strong relationship also goes a long way. However, a dysfunctional family model that leverages threats, anger, or guilt, or the presence of codependent relationships or mental health disorders results in distrust. Problematic family dynamics are common in an eating disordered family, and in that case, compulsion or coercion can lead to long-term resentment and damage to the family unit.

Ethically, explaining the risks and benefits of treatment in a way that can be understood, and providing clear choices is a good approach. However, in the case of cognitive deficiency or incapacity, this may be impossible. Providing choices (all of which are acceptable) is a Love & Logic principle that may be used. I was given the choice of whether to do the intensive inpatient bedfast treatment, design my own treatment, or walk out. Through the grace of God, I selected what I did and am alive today.

Society naturally looks for a quick fix or magic pill, but there isn't one for eating disorders. The thoughts, experiences, and emotions that support an eating disorder will not go away quickly. One of the most important elements of recovery is having caregivers that believe in your ability to recover. When Dr. K. described the intensive inpatient treatment program to me, and told me that if I followed it exactly, I *would* get well, I believed him. There was no maybe, it was simply cause and effect. I remembered his words when I had chest pain, nosebleeds, stomach aches, headaches, or fear. When it was just me alone with my disease, I trusted the words of my doctor. I knew that God was working through him to bring me back to life.

I can do all this through him who gives me strength.

Philippians 4:13 NIV

Treatment Setting and Approach

Close to 10 percent of patients treated for anorexia nervosa drop out of voluntary treatment programs within two weeks. An even higher number are readmitted for treatment four or more times. Despite those disturbing odds, there is a critical window of three years from the time anorexia begins when treatment is most likely to be effective. This is one of many reasons why it is very important for the person with anorexia to enter a treatment program early. A person who gets treatment at an early age, can select food and maintain target weight, successfully eats out on passes, and does not purge (whether the behavior was present before or not) is more likely at five years to retain the weight and be closer to their ideal weight.

Treatment approaches vary. Many who have experienced incest, rape, sexual abuse, or assault find a punitive environment familiar and even comfortable. Despite that, punishment should be avoided. Treatment methods that use punishment to enforce change can seem reasonable and promising, but recovery will not be sustained. Treatment goals should include learning new ways to manage stress, realizing the isolating nature of the disease, and exploring the perceived benefits of disordered eating. The setting should be cooperative rather than competitive. People with anorexia must learn to trust their ability to make the right choices, rather than having others make choices for them. Personal empowerment is essential. Treatment methods that forbid symptoms rather than discussing them will result in only temporary change. Dieting is a practice that promotes temporary behavior changes in an attempt to create lasting change. It rarely reveals or treats the underlying issues that cause dysfunctional eating behavior. Addressing the underlying issues increases the likelihood of lasting change.

Treatment settings and methods that promote shared decision-making, collaboration, personal empowerment, and active involvement support successful partial or full recovery from anorexia nervosa. Conversely, settings that use punishment, hostility, disempowerment, distrust, and dictatorship may fail immediately, or appear successful in the short-term but ultimately fail.

Treatment should be individualized and tailored to the person's acceptance of the disease. For example, weighing oneself is a compulsive behavior shared by most people with anorexia. Ironically, it is also a repetitive and important practice in recovery. Some people with anorexia should stand facing the scale where they can see the numbers, while others should stand facing away.

Anorexia is an enigmatic disease. Treating providers require skill, flexibility, and a collaborative spirit. A phased approach to treatment includes stabilizing and restoring homeostasis, promoting physical and psychological recovery, and reinstating personal autonomy.

The stabilization phase focuses on stabilizing medical problems, and introducing the treatment program. The criteria for inpatient treatment varies between providers and facilities, but often includes weighing less than 70 percent of the ideal weight, BMI around 14 percent, unstable vital signs (bradycardia defined as about 40 heartbeats per minute, arrhythmias, hypotension, hypothermia), electrolyte abnormalities, and dehydration.

An initial step in attaining homeostasis is refeeding. However, with deficiencies of potassium, magnesium, phosphate, zinc, calcium, and vitamins B, C, D, E, and K, refeeding carries its own risks. The longer a person has anorexia, the greater amount of weight lost, and severity of electrolyte imbalance, the higher possibility of morbidity and mortality. Starving yourself right before accepting treatment is a common practice in anorexia nervosa. It is a last-ditch effort to hold on to the disease. Minimal intake for five to 10 days immediately prior to refeeding contributes to the risk of medical complications or death.

Refeeding syndrome signs and symptoms include transient pretibial edema (swelling in the front of the lower leg, often a sign of heart failure), pancreatitis, renal failure, urinary tract infection, and hypokalemia (causing heart palpitations, muscle spasms, and cramping). A history of substance (diuretics, laxatives, cannabis, or alcohol) abuse increases the risk of complications and death during the refeeding phase. The typical onset of refeeding syndrome is hours to three days, and the risks remain for up to 10 days. There are several methods of refeeding, but all require close monitoring and gradually increasing caloric intake through meals and snacks. Other methods include adding high-protein oral liquid supplements, nasogastric (NG) feedings, or as a last resort, intravenous (IV) nutrition. In general, the least intrusive, closest to "normal" refeeding method should be used.

Forced IV or NG feedings can move a person with anorexia from a life-threatening state to a state where they are amenable to treatment. However, initial lifesaving forced treatment should be followed by close monitoring and intensive psychological therapy to help the person accept treatment. If acceptance does not occur, the probability of long-term recovery is low.

Thiamine deficiency (as seen in alcohol dependence), and rapid fluid shifts occur in refeeding and add to potential complications. Fluid and sodium levels must be monitored closely to avoid fluid overload. Signs and symptoms experienced in refeeding include hot flashes, feelings of abdominal fullness and bloating, abdominal cramping, anxiety, and confusion.

Undoubtedly, once the person with anorexia is sufficiently hydrated and nourished, they will be present in the moment and able to hear and process what they are being told, even if they do not agree with it. Intense and frequent counseling should begin immediate and ongoing. The weight-maintenance phase of treatment focuses on increasing caloric intake and conserving energy output to support weight gain. Providing several meals and snacks to a person on bedrest is an example of this.

Unfortunately, in most cases the psychological, emotional, social, and especially spiritual aspects of recovery get less attention as they are more subjective, and assessment instruments are less conclusive. I know that the over-arching, yet least likely to be addressed aspect is spiritual. I know first-hand that God heals. He can heal you with the blink of an eye.

---

*Now faith is confidence in what we hope for
and assurance about what we do not see.*

Hebrews 11:1-3 NIV

My treatment included isolation therapy. I was left alone with the disease, forced to face the illness. I landed in a place of complete surrender, but now I wasn't surrendering to anorexia, I was surrendering anorexia to God. I wrote prayers and letters, and when I was too spent from that, I just lay there and prayed. Journaling and writing therapeutic letters were part of my treatment plan. In them I confessed to God and other people, asked for forgiveness, prayed, and disclosed all my secrets. My catharsis was writing. I spilled all my secrets onto pages and pages until I was sobbing and exhausted, and then I fell into a relieved sleep. Some letters were sent and others were not, but all of them were read by my psychologist.

I had no contact with family or friends for at least a month. The presence, words, and behaviors of the people closest to you often serve to trigger symptoms and feed the disease. Instead, it's crucial that the person with anorexia has the objective support and reassurance of a mental health professional. Anorexia nervosa is a disease of secrecy. The anorectic thoughts and feelings are kept inside, internalized, where they eat away at their prey in privacy. Once the disease is uncovered, as with many addictions, some of the appeal of having an eating disorder goes away. I saw this truth demonstrated in patients with bulimia. Part of the treatment for bulimia was confronting the behavior of vomiting. At meals, snacks, and any time they appeared to be anxious, a nurse would ask them if they wanted to vomit. If they said yes, the nurse would go with them to the bathroom, and talk with them while holding their hair back.

> The Lord is near to all who call on him,
> to all who call on him in truth.
>
> Psalm 145:18 NIV

Medications and Manipulation

Antidepressant, anti-anxiety, and antipsychotic medications are not recommended to treat anorexia nervosa (especially before attaining normal weight) for good reason. They are not proven effective to restore weight, decrease anxiety, or improve depression. This may be in part due to the manipulative and secretive behaviors of anorexia which result in noncompliance. People with anorexia require constant monitoring. Medications will simply not be taken unless the person *wants* to take them. They will be pocketed, flushed, hidden, crushed, or otherwise eliminated in whatever manner available. When I was hospitalized in Carson Hospital, I played games with Valium. I simply didn't take the medication unless I wanted to take it. I wasn't ready to surrender the disease and submit to treatment.

Contrary to that, in City Hospital I was given small med cups of vitamins and minerals several times a day, and I took them all. I had surrendered the disease and accepted help, so there was no need for psychopharmaceuticals, and no reason to fight the help that God had provided for me through the medical professionals. That being said, if anxiety, depression, or obsessive-compulsive disorder are present post-recovery, medications can decrease those symptoms and help prevent relapse.

Trust should be earned. The person with anorexia will not only pocket medications, but also tuck food away, just like a person struggling with alcohol abuse hides the bottle.

Manipulation spawns manipulation. Years of practice results in proficiency. The more I believed I had gotten away with, the more I did. It is important to confront deceitful behavior early, in a firm yet compassionate way. Name the behavior. Describe it and tell the person that you know it is happening, and you know why. Give reasons why the behavior needs to change. Learn what the person with anorexia values. It might be family, friends, boyfriends, clothes, material possessions, or their future. Provide rationale for recovery based on that. Don't treat them like a child even though they look and act like one. Manipulative behaviors thrive in a permissive environment.

Verbal encouragement such as promising the patient that they will look "better," or any comments about their appearance are not advised. Those comments are turned inside-out and heard as observations that they are getting fat. Instead, provide information about the changes to be expected as the body recovers and reawakens. Stay objective and avoid getting emotional. Early in the disease, the anger, sadness, and anxiety of others provides secondary gain in the attention that the person with anorexia craves. Later in the disease, the unbridled emotions of others as they cry only supports the overwhelming guilt the person with anorexia already feels, and causes them to retreat further inside themselves.

Once the person with anorexia is able to process information, treatment should focus on the psychological and emotional aspects of the illness. One-on-one counseling with a qualified therapist should be frequent and ongoing. Discuss the past and how it has led to the present using techniques such as psychodrama. Encourage them to change their life and leave the past behind. Deep inside, they want to. People with anorexia nervosa don't want to die, and they don't want to continue punishing themselves for events and circumstances they hardly remember. If the disease is allowed to progress, the underlying reasons for it fade, and the habitual obsessive-compulsive behaviors strengthen and thrive. Actions, reactions, and mannerisms continue because they seem safe. They provide comfort. The person with anorexia must be willing to let go of them and change their life. Provide encouragement and empower the person. Help them believe that, with God, they have the ability to direct their future. Cognitive-behavioral therapy challenges the distorted, inaccurate thoughts and beliefs that result in harmful behaviors. This type of therapy can help specifically with perfectionism, compulsive behavior, night-eating syndrome, and poor self-esteem.

> I will lift up my eyes to the mountains — where does my help come from? My help comes from the Lord, the Maker of heaven and earth.
>
> Psalm 121:1-2 NIV

Self-hypnosis

Albeit controversial, in my experience self-hypnosis builds confidence. The person with anorexia desperately wants to feel like they can control something…anything. They were able to master their body and starve themselves close to death. Now they must realize that they can bring themselves back to a state of health without becoming obese. Self-hypnosis builds self-confidence because it teaches that through the power of the mind, a person can slow their heartbeat, improve blood circulation, and alter other natural processes. It's important for a person with anorexia to understand that while the thoughts, emotions, and behaviors of others are not within their control, they have the ability to cope with them. Belief in oneself does not conflict with belief in God. God is in control of everything, no matter what. He gave us freedom of choice. Choose to have confidence in the incredible human being that God created you to be, and move forward with your life.

> But he said to me, "My grace is sufficient for you, for my power is made perfect in weakness." Therefore I will boast all the more gladly about my weaknesses, so that Christ's power may rest on me. That is why, for Christ's sake, I delight in weaknesses, in insults, in hardships, in persecutions, in difficulties. For when I am weak, then I am strong.
>
> 2 Corinthians 12: 9-10 (NIV)

Relearning How to Eat

The person with anorexia should initially be allowed to make their own food and drink choices, as this reveals feared or "forbidden" foods and food groups. Not surprisingly, for a person with anorexia, fresh vegetables and most types of fruit are "allowed." Meat, breads, desserts, and milk products are often avoided or forbidden. If they agree to confront the feared foods, provide standard, well-balanced meals. Supervise a person with anorexia at mealtimes because if they are not ready to accept treatment, food will be hidden, flushed, or otherwise will vanish. Do not leave them alone after a meal because for many, anorexia can flip to bulimia in a heartbeat.

Talk to the person with anorexia about bulimia, bulimiarexia, bingeing, purging, fasting, fad diets, drunkorexia, and the delusional thinking that surrounds obsessions about personal ingestion and elimination. If a person with anorexia feels like life is out of control, they will control the only things they think they can control; ingestion and elimination. Similar to a child learning to potty-train, the person with an eating disorder clings to any behavior that makes them feel in control.

The impact of a person's secretive behavior spills over into their relationships. Ingestion and elimination disorders affect the ability to regulate moods. Other people recognize that something is wrong, even though they may not know what. Relationships turn dysfunctional, codependent, or simply break. If you do nothing to conquer an eating disorder, you may end up alone. Face your behavior and understand that it is dysfunctional. See a qualified therapist and talk about it. Take it out of the closet and into the light. Then get out of your comfort zone and take control of your life. Even if you fail, do it again and again until it becomes your lifestyle. I'm not saying this is easy, but I am saying it is possible. Pray to God for help. He is already at the door to help you. Open the door and ask Him into your heart.

Many with anorexia have gone years to decades without eating a standard meal, in public, while seated, or in other normal circumstances. They often need to relearn socially acceptable eating habits. While this is easy to suggest, it is terrifying to change the deeply ingrained habits that have been supported by fear and anxiety for so long.

Exposure therapy is an effective way to decrease the avoidant and ritualistic behavior and irrational fears seen in anorexia nervosa. Unfounded fears include social eating, fear of fat or calories in your food, or loss of control while eating. Instead of facing their fears, people with anorexia will avoid them. They will accept only very small portions, leave food on the plate, or impose strict timing and duration rules around when to eat or drink. These avoidant practices instantly decrease anxiety and give back a false sense of control.

Deluded beliefs support the rituals that are performed to decrease anxiety. Ritualistic behavior includes cutting food up into small pieces, scraping or cleaning off sauces on food, eating and drinking very slowly, manipulating or dissecting food, counting food items, fidgeting, pacing (to burn calories), and constantly tallying calories. People with anorexia are often paranoid, believing that people are watching and judging what, when, and how much they eat.

Exposure therapy identifies the food, drink, and situations eliciting the delusions, fears, and rituals, and enables the person with anorexia to confront them in a safe environment. Repeated exposure to the source of fear naturally decreases anxiety over time. This therapeutic modality is designed to stimulate anxiety and fear, and then coach and guide a person through it. For example, a person with anorexia is given a sandwich with meat, lettuce, tomatoes and mayonnaise. In the first session, the person may only pull out the lettuce and eat it. The therapist will ask what she is thinking and feeling, and confront irrational thoughts. In the next session, the person may cut the sandwich up into several pieces and eat one piece, while the therapist continues to confront the behavior and provide encouragement. After several sessions, the sandwich will simply be eaten.

The person with anorexia will dread exposure therapy sessions, but if this therapy persists, gradual deconditioning will naturally occur. Fear and anxiety decrease to a manageable level and may even go away all together. Confronting the source of fear and anxiety real-time for many times convinces a person that the feared consequence of uncontrollable weight gain will not occur when the ritualistic behavior stops. During therapy, the person with anorexia is also encouraged to discuss their belief that they are being watched while they eat.

Exposure therapy performed in a controlled and monitored setting is effective in treating anorexia nervosa, but the positive effects are not immediate. It is important to monitor the person for a period of time after each session because anxiety can result in a return to the usual practices, which can escalate to the point of deliberate self-harm.

> Then they brought him a demon-possessed man who was blind and mute, and Jesus healed him, so that he could both talk and see.
>
> Matthew 12:22 (NIV)

Psychodrama Explained

Psychodrama is group therapy that uncovers secrets and past experiences contributing to the development and maintenance of eating disorders. The focus is on revealing and exploring distorted thoughts, seeing oneself through another's eyes, and uncovering inner turmoil. With this insight, the person with anorexia can process new ways to manage the disease.

Psychodrama leverages Gestalt therapy to teach mindfulness and focus on the present. As anorexia worsens, so does the ability to identify one's own feelings. To increase awareness, the therapist encourages discussion about thoughts and feelings. Participants dramatize their own psychological conflicts or the conflicts of others through role-reversal, soliloquy, mirroring, doubling, and other techniques. Role-playing is done by assuming the position of your younger self or another person, and serves to increase empathy. Reliving past experiences helps make sense of them and enables expression and resolution of repressed feelings. The therapist may explore the person's dreams, describing them as a reflection of the subconscious mind.

When adding psychodrama or other group therapy, it's important to be aware that people with anorexia learn harmful behaviors from others. Ideas for how to lose weight, eat, not eat, exercise, and otherwise support the dysfunctional thoughts and behaviors that they rely on are gathered in secret. Also, due to the competitive nature of people with anorexia, those who are not ready to surrender the disease desire to be the thinnest or the sickest of the group as a way to gain the most attention.

When the person with anorexia is recovering, they will be prepared to hear and see the value of group meetings like psychodrama. They may say to themselves, "I don't want to be like that." They will look on others with new eyes, and see frightening traits similar to their own which can be very motivating.

Treatment Challenges

The residential phase of treatment supports increasing autonomy. Like every other phase, compliance is voluntary. At first, I was allowed out of bed, and then out of my room. Then I could go to group therapy, the dining room, and other common areas on my own. Soon after, I was playing pool with other residents. As long as I was able to maintain the weight I had gained, I could walk around inside and eventually leave the facility for short periods of time.

Leaving the hospital was terrifying at first. I was allowed to go for walks with a gal a little older than me who had bulimia. The time spent out walking gradually increased to three hours when the weather was nice. Treatment of anorexia includes resuming a healthy level of physical activity. I knew that she struggled with this new freedom as much as I did because we talked about it as we walked. Like people who struggle with other addictions, we were accountable to each other. We discussed our challenges, struggles, and successes, and then went back to the hospital as instructed. I was ready to move past anorexia and shut the door behind me. I knew God had healed me for a purpose, and the desire to fulfill my purpose was stronger than anything else.

A hospital stay is expensive for everyone. An intensive inpatient treatment program can cost tens of thousands of dollars, which explains why there are very few public programs like these. It's important to stress how a patient with an eating disorder needs intensive therapy for a period of time long enough to recover both physically and psychologically. New habits must be taught, practiced, and reinforced. This often takes between two and nine months. The duration must depend on what it takes to achieve physical and mental health stability and recovery to the greatest extent possible. People with anorexia live a life of avoidance. Exposure to forbidden, feared food and activity in a controlled supportive environment helps the patient face her greatest terrors in a safe place.

Treatment done in an inpatient setting can address all facets of the disease. Social anxiety can be overpowered by being with other people. Habitual solitude and secrecy can be made ineffective by telling all in a shared, open environment. Forbidden and feared food and beverages can be made less ominous by having them on the menu, and serving them at mealtime. Compulsive exercise can be controlled by living in a structured, predictable environment. Per my experience, a temporary inpatient setting is essential to beating an eating disorder. A halfway approach such as a partial day program is far less likely to be successful because it allows anorexia nervosa to thrive outside of those hours.

Unfortunately, insurance companies rarely cover a prolonged inpatient stay for an eating disorder diagnosis unless it has resulted in a significant and dangerous decline in physical health, or the person is a danger to themselves or others. Even then, the goal is short-term stabilization rather than long-term recovery. People with anorexia know that remaining in or returning to an environment that was conducive to illness will only continue supporting the illness. A partial treatment program only allows freedom for the disease to proliferate during non-treatment hours. This system does not address the complexity of the disease or all the ways it can control and ruin your life.

Carry each other's burdens, and in this way
you will fulfill the law of Christ.

Galatians 6:2 (NIV)

Perseverance

Anorexia may go away, but personality traits that coincide with anorexia do not. I am still competitive, insecure, self-conscious, anxious, and often have a negative body image, 30 years post-recovery.

I continue to be a perfectionist with my work and hobbies. These traits have caused problems in my adult life. I went back to school to obtain a bachelor's and then a master's degree. Afraid that my work was not good enough, I'd stay up well into the night perfecting assignments and papers, until the online submission deadline was minutes away and I was forced to release the work for grading. A psychologist once suggested that I submit a paper at 10 p.m. instead of the 2 a.m. deadline, just to see what happens; would I be graded differently than if I stayed up for another four hours perfecting it?

This "exposure therapy" challenged my belief that the assignments must be "perfect," even though they would never reach my goal of absolute perfection. After much angst and convincing, I finally agreed to submit a (less important) assignment at 10 p.m., and found that I was given the same grade as I had for assignments that I had spent hours longer on! The best example of trait persistence in my life is this book. I knew I would write it, but I have sat on the project for three decades. I believe that God will take it now and use it to fulfill His will in people's lives — maybe your life.

Negative body image precludes anorexia and remains even after treatment. After I was discharged from the hospital, part of my treatment plan was to sculpt clay figures. I was asked to create a "normal" woman (that I wanted to look like), and a second woman that I feared I would look like. I labored over the figures until I thought they resembled the images in my mind. Both women were lying on their sides in red dresses. The normal woman was slim with a sexy, pear-shaped figure. The second woman was obese, with an apple shape and rolls of extra fat. Looking at the sculptures helped me understand my ideal and feared body shapes. My psychologist explained that my ideal body was within my reach, and if I wanted it bad enough, I could achieve and maintain it. I recommend art therapy using clay or another medium to help a person with anorexia better understand distorted body image, and realize that she has the ability to manage and control her own weight and appearance.

Some studies show that chronic dieters have eight times the risk of developing an eating disorder than those do not. Chronic dieters have issues with impulsiveness, and lack concentration and motivation. On the other hand, chronic dieters share many of the same traits as people with eating disorders, including drive for thinness, body dissatisfaction, warped body image, low self-esteem, depression, and difficulty adapting to change. The greater the dissatisfaction and pursuit of thinness, the greater the dietary restraint.

Psychological vulnerability is another feature we share. Chronic dieters and women prone to eating disorders are suggestible and easily swayed. We are more apt to use control over eating or food itself as a coping mechanism. We tend to be conformists and people-pleasers. Add self-centeredness, depression, low self-esteem, a strong desire to belong and be loved, perfectionism, competitiveness and history of abuse or a trigger event, and all the ingredients for an eating disorder are present. These attributes increase the risk of attracting or being attracted to people who are entitled, lack empathy, and are interpersonally exploitive. Prayer and counseling can help a person with anorexia develop discernment, which can save them from a future of frustration and heartbreak in their relationships.

Prepubertal onset, short duration of disease, and early treatment result in a better treatment outcome. Despite this, people who have lived with anorexia nervosa for a long time, or who appear to have intractable anorexia should not give up hope. The most effective treatment measures for this population are nourishing the body and participating in anorexia nervosa specific psychotherapy. The longer you have anorexia, the more likely you will develop comorbid psychiatric and medical disorders and die of the disease. Treatment goals that include improved quality of life versus recovery might be considered for the adult or person with chronic anorexia. I mention this reluctantly because God healed me, and He can heal you no matter how old you are or how long you have struggled with anorexia nervosa. He is waiting for you to ask Jesus into your heart, and to surrender the disease. I promise you that He will lift it from you if you let go of it.

Therefore, if anyone is in Christ, the new creation has come: The old has gone, the new is here!

2 Corinthians 5:17 (NIV)

Relapse

Some studies show that close to 80 percent of those with anorexia nervosa partially recover, and close to one-third seem to fully recover. However, almost half of these people relapse. A person with anorexia who participates in outpatient, structured, cognitive-behavioral therapy post-discharge is less likely to relapse within the first year than one who does not.

My hospital discharge criteria was to attain a certain weight (110 lbs.), resume menses, gain insight into my illness, be able to self-select the appropriate types and amounts of food, and maintain the weight I had gained even with exercising. I achieved the weight goals and greater insight into my problem but did not start menstruating. (Menstruation criteria has since been omitted from anorexia nervosa treatment guidelines.) I also had not fully overcome the disorder psychologically and because of that, I relapsed. The fear of fatness was still there. Once I left the hospital I felt like a bird let out of a cage. I had ongoing outpatient visits with my psychologist weekly, and less frequently over time. I realized that anorexia still had a grip on me, but God held me tighter.

Returning to school and the memories, people, reminders, and environment that sustained anorexia was hard, but I felt confident and powerful knowing that God had a plan and purpose for me, and it did not include anorexia. I feared that being back home would trigger anorexia and despite my new hope, I fought that fear every day. Evidence supports that the distress and behavior of parents or caregivers inadvertently maintains the disease. Sensing this, I did all I could, as fast as I could, to graduate high school and leave. The day after graduation, I moved to my grandma's house, one hundred miles away. She traveled the world and at that time was on a trip overseas. I busied myself as much as I could with part-time jobs dunking donuts and cooking bacon (I still hate donuts and bacon), until learning that I had been accepted into university in the Fine Arts program in the same city where I had been hospitalized just months before.

Now out on my own, I religiously followed the instructions given by the hospital discharge team for diet and exercise for five or six months and maintained the weight I had gained, but then started slipping back into my old, familiar, and well-established, unforgotten habits. Most of us know from personal experience that it is far easier to change a habit than to maintain that change over time. I found ways and times to increase my exercise. I started dating an attractive, athletic man who appreciated my body, and I put more pressure on myself to look like the woman I thought he wanted to see. My focus was still on outward appearance even though now I knew God lived in my heart. Besides walking and running, I added swimming and ballroom dancing. Twenty pounds came off easily within a few months. No matter how you slice it, that's called a relapse. This is when the fistula obtained from the decubitus ulcer from being on bedrest got infected. That fistula helped me see that I was standing on the edge of a slippery slope. A few more poor choices and I would rapidly fall right back to anorexia, waiting for me with open arms.

Circumstances contributing to the risk of relapse include force-feeding and agreeing to treatment to pacify parents or others. Some studies show that people who do not meet discharge criteria and/or have an additional diagnosis such as anxiety, substance use, major depression, or bipolar disorder are more likely to relapse. Research also shows that the continued practice of disordered eating behavior including food restrictions or rituals, bingeing and purging (vomiting or use of laxatives), and deliberate self-injury are associated with higher likelihood of relapse. Although I felt the peace beyond understanding that only comes from God, anxiety lay in hiding, and the renewed style of eating that I had adopted had not yet become a way of life.

My relapse happened nine months after I was discharged from the hospital. When I realized that a relapse was happening, I made the choice to remember what God had done for me. He had saved my life. I had been released from the bondage of anorexia and had tasted the freedom of young adulthood, and I loved it. In appreciation of what He had done for me, I turned back to God.

My dad had given me a fuzzy white blanket years before. I put that blanket on the floor in the corner of my dorm room and sat there for a while every day, reading my Bible. Whenever I felt anxiety or sadness, I would sit there and read. Soon, I began to remember and think about the word of God even when I wasn't sitting there, and comfort would fall like a blanket over me. This got me through each day, and over time, I regained self-confidence as well as the weight I had lost. Without God, I would have allowed anorexia to take me again. I was not and am not strong enough to fight off anorexia without God.

Relapse

Rend your heart and not your garments. Return to the Lord your God, for he is gracious and compassionate, slow to anger and abounding in love, and he relents from sending calamity.

Joel 2:13 (NIV)

Parenting and Eating Disorders

Refusing food asserts control over an environment that otherwise seems out of control. At a very young age, children learn that parents can be controlled with their eating behavior. Picking up the Cheerios that your toddler throws reinforces the child's discovery and delight that a parent can be controlled though behavior involving food. Early signs of eating psychopathology can lead to disordered eating practices at a later age. Force-feeding and overfeeding infants can decrease or eliminate their ability to recognize and interpret signs of fullness. This increases the risk of obesity. Fussy eating in children often gets attention from parents (especially parents with current or history of eating disorders). Even negative attention is perceived as better than no attention, thus rewarding the behavior and making it more likely to continue.

Studies show that parents of adult children with history of eating disorders asserted control over the child's eating behavior at an earlier age than parents of children without eating disorders. Learn physical cues that your infant is satisfied and respect those cues. Teach children how to recognize they are hungry or full. All of us are born with this ability but many ignore it. Baby sign language is a good way to communicate with a non-verbal infant or young child. With it, a young child can tell you when they have eaten enough.

Confront moodiness and teach children the relationship between moods and blood sugar. Challenge bad habits early, such as skipping meals during the day and bingeing at night. These habits are very hard to break and can be disabling for years and even decades. Don't use food or drink as a reward or punishment, or to show love. Don't draw attention to food as this elevates the importance of food and fosters dysfunctional eating practices. Don't use guilt to attempt to control eating behavior. The child with an eating disorder feels bad enough about themselves as it is; adding guilt only worsens anorexia. In my case, I knew my eating habits were dysfunctional. Early in the disorder, they provided the attention I craved, but later I realized how my behavior was affecting other people and I felt guilt and shame. At that point, anorexia controlled me and it was stronger than what I was feeling. When Mom used guilt (whether consciously or subconsciously) to try to change my behavior, I simply shut down. I didn't have the energy or desire to engage in that emotional train ride with her, or any emotion really, with anyone.

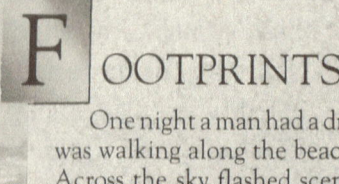

FOOTPRINTS

One night a man had a dream. He dreamed he was walking along the beach with the Lord. Across the sky flashed scenes from his life. For each scene, he noticed two sets of footprints in the sand: one belonging to him, and the other to the Lord.

When the last scene of his life flashed before him, he looked back at the footprints in the sand. He noticed that many times along the path of his life there was only one set of footprints. He also noticed that it happened at the very lowest and saddest times in his life.

This really bothered him and he questioned the Lord about it. "Lord, You said that once I decided to follow You, You'd walk with me all the way. But I have noticed that during the most troublesome times in my life, there is only one set of footprints. I don't understand why when I needed You most You would leave me."

The Lord replied, "My son, My precious child, I love you and would never leave you. During your times of trial and suffering, when you see only one set of footprints, it was then that I carried you."

Author Unknown

I have a ring on my right hand middle finger. It is three bands intertwined. Each band is different. They are gold, white gold, and pink gold. Someone once called it a "wish ring." After I got out of the hospital at age 18, my mom took me shopping and bought this ring for me. This ring was to be a promise that I would never get sick again. I am not sure if it was intended to be a promise to me, my mom, both of us, or God. Except for during and right after surgeries, I have not taken it off. When the anorexia thoughts crossed my mind after I was released from the hospital, this ring was a reminder. As I look at it now, 30 years later, it is still a reminder of what could have happened, and to thank God for my life. I have had three wedding bands come and go, but my tri-gold ring will stay on my finger forever.

God worked through my mom. She was the impetus for me to surrender anorexia. When she finally let go of me by telling me that she couldn't help me anymore, I realized that it was *my choice* to surrender the disease. I wasn't doing it for her or anyone else; I was doing it for me. I realized that I was a young adult, able to choose my own path. I owe Mom my life. She was the influencing factor to my career as a nurse. I owe her my career. She was a caring mom and cared enough to let me go. Later in life, she taught me how to be a mom.

All parents have several things in common; we have all screwed up. We could have been better parents. We all have regrets. We all blame ourselves for the choices our kids made that end up in disaster. I have reminders of the fruits of the Spirit posted where I can see them every day, and although I consistently fail to maintain them, they are perfect to apply in parenting. As a parent, we must do our very best with this awesome responsibility that God has given us, but we must also accept and forgive ourselves for the mistakes we make, pray for God to help us stop making them, and move forward.

"But the fruit of the Spirit is love, joy, peace, forbearance, kindness, goodness, faithfulness, gentleness and self-control. Against such things there is no law."

Galatians 5:22-25 (NIV)

The majority of women with a history or presence of eating disorders have parenting difficulties and feelings of inadequacy. Anorexia survivors live with low self-esteem lurking just below the surface. If a woman with anorexia is able to get pregnant and is blessed with a child, raising it can trigger eating disorder behavior and exacerbate symptoms. Recognizing this and intervening with prayer is essential. God knows your weakness and if you ask, He will fill your gaps. Involve other supportive people to teach you how to parent. In my case, I grabbed hold of the Love and Logic parenting philosophy and dug in, hoping that it would help me learn all that I lacked. Eating disordered parents who have accepted their diagnosis and made efforts to recover, fear that their children will grow up with eating disorders. Although a parent who has recovered from an eating disorder may not ask for help to parent their children, inside they are begging for it.

Studies show that the shorter the duration of anorexia, the younger a person with anorexia gets treatment, and meeting full discharge criteria increases the likelihood that recovery will endure long-term. It is important that parents take charge. Confront the dysfunctional behavior, and plant and water the seeds of recovery. Understand how and why your child developed and suffers with an eating disorder, and accept responsibility for your part in it. Parental concern is often expressed as hypervigilance (Love & Logic calls this helicopter parenting). Do not coddle the child. Do not blame yourself, others, the circumstances, situation, or environment for anorexia nervosa. Do not believe that you or the child are victims. This attitude of helplessness only feeds the eating disorder. Empower your child to overcome it, and then step back and let them.

Mothers who are overly concerned with eating and

weight, and use outward appearance to measure self-worth are far more likely to raise children with eating disorders or disordered eating. Comments made by either a father or mother about weight and eating significantly impact a child's dieting behaviors and self-perception. The more frequent these comments, the greater the child's body weight dissatisfaction and dieting behaviors. As a parent, increase your awareness of what you say and how often you comment on your weight or your child's weight. Your obsession with food and weight does not go unheard. Children hear and see a lot more than we think they do. Whether subconsciously or consciously, you are planting the seed in your child that can easily grow into an eating disorder.

Relax at mealtimes and model healthy eating and a balanced diet. Then put the food away. Even though our society is very food-centric, frame eating as necessary for life; don't let life revolve around eating.

Start children off on the way they should go, and when they are older they will not turn from it.

Proverbs 22:6 (NIV)

Recovery and Growth

Anorexia treatment must address poor self-esteem, shame, and personal punishment. The traits common to those with anorexia nervosa that drove the person to lose tremendous amounts of weight, including stubbornness, perfectionism, competitiveness, perseverance, endurance, drive, rigidity, obsessiveness, compulsiveness, and high tolerance to pain and fatigue, can be channeled into wellness. Convince the person with anorexia that they are strong enough to accomplish anything, including physical and psychological wellness, achievements, and peace. Convince them that they don't need to change their personality, but rather channel these characteristics into success and wellness. With time, the person with anorexia will start to believe it and pursue health and wellness.

As expected, after weight is restored, the amount of calories needed to sustain it is unpredictable. Some studies show that significantly more calories than expected are necessary, whereas other studies have found that metabolism slows and fewer calories are needed. Much like being released from prison, everything seemed unpredictable outside of the confines of the hospital. I craved predictability and reliability in order to continue progressing to wellness. I feared slipping back to anorectic habits as much as becoming overweight or obese. I also knew that God had plans for me, and I needed to be well in order to fulfill them. I had to let go of the tendency to count calories in everything I consumed, and instead adhere to a semi-structured meal plan. I also practiced listening to my body and eating when I was hungry, in the amount needed to feel satisfied.

Some experts believe that the duration a person has anorexia nervosa should be equal to the duration of treatment. I had anorexia for three years, and participated in therapy for three years afterwards. Ongoing psychological treatment should continue past weight restoration for at least a year, and as long as five or six years to combat the persistent thoughts and behaviors of anorexia. Even decades post-recovery it's important to recognize when stress builds up, and seek help.

The longer a person has anorexia, the more likely there will be an effect on the brain. Research supports a loss of gray matter leading to depression, anxiety, rigid thought processes, and a tendency toward social withdrawal. The effects on the brain make it obvious that malnutrition must be treated and reversed before psychological treatment can even begin. Studies show that effects on the brain can be reversed (brain volume restored) with a minimum of three years of consistent, adequate nutrition. The personality that existed before anorexia will reemerge. I had doubts about my own intelligence for decades post-recovery. In an effort to prove myself wrong, I moved forward, furthering my education and accepting challenging jobs to prove to myself that I was in the range of normal intelligence.

Anorexia also ravages bone health, especially if it occurs during adolescence when bones should be growing and strengthening. In my early 20s, I sustained a stress fracture of the tibia. Soon after, I fell and broke bones in my right hand and had a number of broken bones in my toes and foot. These occurred while running and teaching aerobics classes. The fractures prompted a DEXA scan revealing borderline osteoporosis. I was frustrated with myself, but not surprised. In most cases, low bone mineral density is not completely reversible even after weight is restored. I turned my stubborn determination to the end of reversing osteopenia through diet and supplements. Close to ten years after making that choice, my femur density was normal and vertebral density improved.

Anorexia also challenges the endocrine system, specifically the conversion of T4 to T3. This is likely the body's adaptation to starvation by reducing metabolic rate. I have been treated for hypothyroidism for most of my adult life. The disastrous effects of anorexia can color the rest of your life. Calcium, vitamin D, and simply getting enough of all vitamins and minerals is important to me, and I rarely go a day without consuming enough through diet and supplements.

A few short years after recovery, I was working in the hospital as a nurse on the night shift. The night shift on a rehab unit was an awesome opportunity to get to know the patients. One of mine was an obese female who was postop bilateral total knee replacements. She had to lie flat on her back in bed with her legs in continuous passive motion (CPM) machines a few times a day as part of her recovery program. She told me that the knee replacements were required because of carrying her own excess body weight. It seemed that this fact had just become clear to her as she told me about her lifelong struggle with weight. To my surprise, I heard many similarities in our stories. Her clothes didn't fit right and neither did mine. She was anxious before eating, and so was I. She felt guilty after eating, as did I. People glanced at her twice, just as they did with me. I realized that many of us struggle with weight, regardless of whether you are underweight, overweight, or normal weight. I felt blessed to be able to talk to her about my experience with anorexia. I told her that being underweight was not the secret to happiness, as so many think it is. Many people believe that if they could lose weight, their lives would suddenly get easier and better, and they would finally be confident and joyful. Weight loss or gain will not magically make you a happier person. Happiness is a choice.

That being said, staying at a normal weight for your height will help prevent the growing list of health conditions associated with carrying too much weight, including hypertension, high cholesterol, cancer, and diabetes, to name only a few. Reach a normal weight to increase your chance of having a longer life, free of preventable disease. Do not lose weight "to be happy." That late-night discussion with my patient helped me understand that the critical, disapproving, vain, superior attitude I had about people who are overweight had now been replaced with empathy.

Only with the grace of God am I alive to write this book. I am a flawed human being and a work in progress. It has taken me decades to write this book because I was afraid to face my past. A popular Christian song repeats, "Fear is a liar." Fear is not from God. Courage is. In this book, I have shared experiences that changed and colored my life. Many of us stuff these secrets deep inside for years, even decades, like I did. Even when kept secret, the memories are still there. I invite you to write your own story. Doing so will help you make peace with it, and your story can help other people make peace with theirs.

> Yet you, Lord, are our Father. We are the clay, you are the potter; we are all the work of your hand.
>
> Isaiah 64:8 (NIV)

I love the story in the New Testament about the women with the alabaster jar, who washed Jesus' feet with her tears, wiped them with her hair, kissed his feet, and put ointment on them. She had faith, and Jesus said her sins were forgiven. God gave her peace. I have felt this peace, and someday I hope to hear those words.

This book describes only a few times that God has shown me that He is right here, but there have been many more times. God always finds me in my weakest moments, especially when I am anxious about parenting or money. He has worked miracles in my life, and if you ask and believe, He will also work miracles in yours. Step back from your circumstances and notice that for Christians, those are not coincidences. That is God actively working in your life. Life on this Earth is a time-limited gift. What does God want us to do with this gift? Fully experience, appreciate, and enjoy it! Give Him thanks because He is orchestrating all of it for you.

My mouth will tell of your righteous deeds,
of your saving acts all day long—
though I know not how to relate them all.
I will come and proclaim your mighty acts, Sovereign Lord;
I will proclaim your righteous deeds, yours alone.
Since my youth, God, you have taught me,
and to this day I declare your marvelous deeds.
Even when I am old and gray,
do not forsake me, my God,
till I declare your power to the next generation,
your mighty acts to all who are to come.

Psalm 71: 15-18 (NIV)

---

www.ingramcontent.com/pod-product-compliance
Lightning Source LLC
Chambersburg PA
CBHW030322100526
44592CB00010B/524